52 WEEKS WITH WOMEN OF THE BIBLE

A BIBLE STUDY GUIDE

52 WEEKS WITH WOMEN OF THE BIBLE

Ann Spangler & Jean E. Syswerda

HarperChristian Resources

52 Weeks with Women of the Bible
Copyright © 2026 by Ann Spangler and Jean Syswerda

Published by HarperChristian Resources, 3950 Sparks Drive SE, Suite 101, Grand Rapids, MI 49546, USA.
HarperChristian Resources is a registered trademark of HarperCollins Christian Publishing, Inc.

Requests for information should be addressed to customercare@harpercollins.com.

ISBN 978-0-310-18206-1 (softcover)
ISBN 978-0-310-18207-8 (ebook)

HarperCollins Publishers, Macken House, 39/40 Mayor Street Upper, Dublin 1, D01 C9W8, Ireland (https://www.harpercollins.com).

Art Direction: Ron Huizinga
Cover Design: Michelle Lenger
Interior Design: Sarah Johnson
Photo Credits: Ann Spangler photograph © Dan Davis Photography,
Jean E. Syswerda photograph © Jessica Jones

First Printing June 2026 / Printed in the United States of America

CONTENTS

INTRODUCTION

When we first wrote about women of the Bible more than twenty-five years ago, hardly anything on the market was solely devoted to the topic. Our book, *Women of the Bible: A One-Year Devotional Study*, which has been revised and updated since then, was primarily designed to serve as a daily devotional guide. The book was for people who were eager to delve into stories about the lives of women who lived in ways foreign and yet familiar as they struggled with issues common to our own world.

Now, we have written another book that is primarily focused on study. Though the original book provides solid background information, *52 Weeks with Women of the Bible* invites readers to probe the text even more deeply. Our hope is that you will discover that the two books, though they can be read independently, together offer a robust program for both devotion and study.

In many ways, we are grateful that we waited so long to write this study because so much helpful scholarship has been published since we first researched the original book. This study is based on some of that research and is designed to help you slow down and savor the text. It does not rush you through Scripture. As you read about the various women week by week, you will discover that their stories don't stand on their own but are connected to the larger biblical narrative. Discovering how they are linked to each other and to the whole story of the Bible is part of the delight of learning about them.

In a day and age overflowing with distractions, we invite you to engage in a weekly rhythm of reading, reflection, and study. We've designed *52 Weeks with Women of the Bible* to be used individually or with others. Groups will find that it provides a flexible structure for discussion, allowing participants to share their understanding and experience in a way that nourishes their love for the Bible and strengthens their sense of community. While the stories are organized in the order in which the women appear in the Bible, that order may be adapted in any way you like. For those who decide to study the women from the first page to the last, the book can serve as a mini commentary, explaining the story of the Bible freshly and uniquely from the perspective of these remarkable women. Though such an abbreviated commentary can't tell you everything you need to know, it can paint the big picture in ways you may not have considered.

To give you a sense that there is a historical progression to what you are reading, we have attempted to date each woman's story. These dates are debatable, especially when it comes to the era of the Patriarchs (Abraham, Isaac, Jacob) and the exodus. In the case of the exodus, there are early and late date frameworks with the former beginning in the mid-fifteenth century BC and the latter beginning about 1270–1250 BC. We have adopted the late-date framework, as that is in line with what most modern scholars think. More important than accurately dating these stories is realizing how significant they are in God's plan of salvation. This is particularly true since the Bible's focus is theological rather than chronological.

In our attempt to write an easy-to-use study informed by solid scholarship, we have been especially helped by the work of Tikva Frymer-Kensky, Ben Witherington III, N. T. Wright, Tim Mackie, and Kenneth Bailey. After writing the book, we came across a wonderful work by Ingrid Faro entitled *Redeeming Eden: How Women in the Bible Advance the Story of Salvation*, more evidence that scholars are looking closely at these stories, which are significant for both men and women. In fact, if you are a woman reading this book, we hope you will share it with the men in your life, as these stories, so rich in meaning, belong to us all.

It has been a joy to revisit this topic in its ancient context. We have been amazed at how each new reading uncovers fresh insights into the wonderful book we call the Bible. Despite our passion for these stories, our certainty of their importance, and our best efforts to write a good book, we realize that no book is perfect, which is why we accept that any deficiencies in this one are solely our responsibility. Whatever these may be, we hope they will not prevent you from learning about the Bible in a way that draws you close to the One who desires to speak to you through all the stories and on every page of Scripture.

Ann Spangler
Jean E. Syswerda

WEEK 1

EVE

"LIFE-GIVING" OR "MOTHER OF ALL WHO HAVE LIFE"

Her Story

The first woman, she was at peace with God, her husband, and herself, until she listened to Satan and doubted God. Adam's perfect partner, she is considered the "mother of all the living."

Adam and his wife were both naked, and they felt no shame. GENESIS 2:25

READ

Genesis 1:26–4:26

Who WAS SHE?

As a creature made in God's image, Eve was meant to be so full of wisdom and life that she could rule the world alongside Adam in a way that manifested God's goodness and love. Instead, she is remembered for believing the lie that broke God's beautiful world. Because of their twin rebellion, both Adam and Eve were cast out of Eden. Even so, God promised that one of Eve's offspring would crush the snake and free creation from its bondage to death. Out of death would come life!

A *Closer Look* AT EVE'S STORY

The Hebrew title for Genesis is *Bereshit*, meaning "in the beginning," a fitting name for a book that sets the stage for everything that follows. Careful reading of Eve's story yields startling insights about the entire Bible and God's intentions at the birth of the universe.

The first chapter leaves no doubt about who human beings are. In just two verses, Scripture tells us four times that we are created in God's image. God places this truth front and center to help us withstand the onslaught of confusion and misery that will descend because of Adam and Eve's disobedience. He also affirms women's full status: "male and female he created them" (Genesis 1:27).

In the first chapters of Genesis, the word *adam* isn't considered a proper name until after Eve is named. Before that it simply means "the human." During and before Jesus' day, the phrase about being created "male and female" was understood by some to mean that the original "adam," or human, was both male and female.

The word translated "rib" in Genesis 1:27 is *tzela*, which could more properly be translated as "side," as in two equal sides of something. Many scholars believe we should imagine God not extracting a rib from Adam to fashion Eve but separating the human into two equal sides to create the first man and woman.[1]

When Genesis was written, people in surrounding cultures believed that the gods implanted their images only in idols or kings. For a divine image to be placed within every human being—even within women—would have been considered incredible. Pagan religions depicted humans as mere tools, designed to serve the gods by performing menial tasks, like fetching food for them. Genesis turns this upside down, portraying God not as a demanding slave master, but as one who cares for and provides. Rather than forcing Adam and Eve to feed him, he provides them with food and a home, placing them in a lush garden paradise.

The garden Genesis describes is like a landscaped paradise with winding paths, fragrant fruit trees, and pools of water. It's

---

1 See John Walton, *The Lost World of Adam and Eve* (IVP Academic, 2015), 78–80, and also Lois Tverberg, "Together Again," Engedi Resource Center, posted on https://engediresourcecenter.com/2015/07/07/together-again/#gsc.tab=0http://www.egrc.net/articles/Rock/Jesus_Jewish_Teachings/Together Again.html).

the kind of elegant garden that would have graced a palace or temple. The implication is clear: God intended Adam and Eve's garden home—and our home too—to be right next to his in the family compound.

How tragic that we lost that privileged place! Was God being mean when he banished Adam and Eve? On the contrary. He was showing incredible mercy. Remaining in Eden would have doomed Eve and her husband to a life of never-ending sin. They would have been able to eat from the Tree of Life, which would have given them immortality. In his wisdom and great love, God expelled them, but not without making a promise. Genesis 3:15 tells us that God planned to give Eve, as the mother of all the living, a descendant who would eventually crush the head of the serpent. Right after the fall, God was already pointing to a way for his children to come home.

EVE'S *Legacy* IN SCRIPTURE

READ

Genesis 2:18–25

- Picture in your mind what life in Eden was like before and then after Adam and Eve disobeyed God. Describe what you see.

- The word *helper* in Genesis 2:18, 20 is the not-too-helpful English translation of the Hebrew word *ezer*, referring to Eve's creation as a partner for Adam. Most often the word *ezer* in the Old Testament refers to God (Exodus 18:4; Deuteronomy 33:7; Psalm 10:14; 27:9; 118:7). A better translation might be "ally" or "delivering ally." How might this use of *ezer* elevate your understanding of your position as a woman?

- Describe how you see "one flesh" (Genesis 2:24) in a marriage lived out in the physical, emotional, and spiritual aspects of life.

READ
Genesis 3

- What desires did Eve have that the serpent offered to fulfill (Genesis 3:5-6)?

- What desires or fears make you vulnerable to temptation?

- From the passage, it appears Adam was present when the serpent tempted Eve (Genesis 3:6). Explore the significance of this.

- When punished after sinning, what new feelings did Eve experience? Look especially at Genesis 3:7-8, 16.

OUR *Connection* TO EVE

Because of our first parents' disobedience, they—and we—suffered the terrible consequences. Seeing the forbidden fruit, they decided that it would be good and not evil to pluck and eat it. Like them, we are still addicted to defining good and evil on our own terms rather than on how God defines it.

- In what ways is the image of God most broken in people today? How do you think God wants to restore his image in us—and in you?

- How does the story of the first human beings provide insight into our world and into your own struggles today?

- Notice that the first lie in the history of the world was about God's character. In John 8:44, Jesus called the devil "a liar and the father of lies." What distortions about God have you been tempted to believe and with what result?

Father, our lives today still reel from the consequences of Satan's lies. Help us as we put on your armor to fight against him. Give us wisdom when we're confronted with choices that draw us away from you, and help us to see the way out of temptation you've promised to provide.

WEEK 2

SARAH

"CHIEFTAINESS" OR "PRINCESS"

Her Story

She laughed at God's promise of a son in her old age. The last laugh was on her when she gave birth at ninety.

Sarah said, "God has brought me laughter, and everyone who hears about this will laugh with me." GENESIS 21:6

READ

Genesis 12; 16:1–10; 17:15–22; 18:1–9; 21:1–7

Who WAS SHE?

Sarah may be one of the few women in history remembered primarily for her laughter. Not a bad epitaph, except she laughed at God. Not *with* God in joy at his promise, but *at* God for the absurdity of it.

In Sarah's story God uses what is humanly impossible to prove to all generations that this new nation, birthed out of old Sarah and even older Abraham, is no accident but part of his eternal plan.

A *Closer Look* AT SARAH'S STORY

HER STORY TOOK PLACE AROUND 2000–1800 BC.

Sarah is a fascinating and complex character. Early in her story, we learn that she and Abraham migrated to Egypt during a severe famine. In many ways the story of their stay in Egypt prefigured the captivity that the Israelites would undergo many years later, when their grandson Jacob and his extended family would be forced to move to Egypt during a multiyear famine.

Because beauty often attracts power, Pharaoh added Sarah to his harem soon after she and Abraham arrived. But God freed her by sending a plague on Pharaoh and his household, foreshadowing how he would one day send plagues to force a far worse pharaoh to let go of the captive Hebrew slaves.

After that, Sarah and Abraham returned home enriched by all the treasure Pharaoh had showered on Abraham in exchange for Sarah. In a strange echo hundreds of years later, the Egyptians heaped treasure on the Israelite slaves as they, too, left Egypt (Exodus 12:35–36).

Sarah was sixty-five when God first promised Abraham a son. But years passed and there was still no baby. Tired of waiting, she decided to move things along by invoking a culturally accepted practice. She suggested to Abraham that he sleep with her maid, Hagar, in hopes that she would bear him an heir.

But this was a subversion of the covenant God had made with Abraham. It led to the abuse and near death of Hagar and her son, Ishmael. Though chosen by God to accomplish his purposes, both Abraham and Sarah fell prey to the same sort of sin that had ensnared Adam and Eve, who had eaten from the Tree of the Knowledge of Good and Evil. This habit of reaching for what looked good in their own eyes, without regard to God, would repeat itself over and over in the story of Scripture.

Sarah, hailed as a hero of the faith in the New Testament (Hebrews 11:11-12), hardly seemed full of heroism when the Lord told Abraham that in a year's time, his eighty-nine-year-old wife would bear him a son. Instead, she laughed.

A hidden note in the story indicates that Sarah may have begun menstruating again. When the three strangers depicted in the story ask after Sarah, Abraham demurs, saying she is "there, in the tent" (Genesis 18:9), a euphemism that could have indicated she had isolated herself in her tent, as was customary for all menstruating women.[2]

Despite her sins and failings, after the birth of her son, Isaac, Sarah couldn't help but laugh at the astonishing goodness of God's plan. Her life is proof of God's willingness to use broken people—and we are all broken—to accomplish his purposes.

---

2 For more on this, see John H. Walton, "Genesis," *Zondervan Illustrated Bible Backgrounds Commentary on the Old Testament*, ed. John H. Walton (Zondervan, 2009), 1:91, and Ann Spangler, *Less Than Perfect* (Zondervan, 2018) 47–49.

Sarah's *Legacy* in Scripture

READ
Genesis 16:1-6

What is your impression of Sarah based on these verses?

READ
Genesis 17:15-17; 18:10-19

Consider these two passages carefully. In Abraham and Sarah's story, her laughter is often highlighted, but Abraham's laughter, not so often. Why? What is different about their laughter?

- In what ways are you like Sarah when something God has promised or a prayer you have been praying for a long time doesn't come to fruition?

READ
Genesis 21:1-7

- God's promise of a son for Sarah and Abraham finally arrived. What does the arrival of Isaac tell you about not only God's faithfulness but his grace?

- Describe how you think laughter played into this story.

OUR *Connection* TO SARAH

When God reaffirmed his covenant with Abraham, he changed Sarai's name to Sarah and then promised that she would bear a son: "I will bless her, and she shall become nations; kings of peoples shall come from her" (Genesis 17:16 ESV). What an amazing promise, given to a woman who was a combination of both light and shadows. Neither all good nor all bad—like most of us. God didn't—and still doesn't—wait for perfection to put his plan into motion.

- God fulfilled his promise to Abraham and Sarah in his time. Why do you think God waited until they were beyond childbearing age to give them a son?

- God worked through Sarah's life despite her failings. How could God use you despite your imperfections?

- Is your current situation more like Sarah's before or after God fulfilled his promises to her? Explain.

- Describe a time in your life when God "brought [you] laughter" (Genesis 21:6).

God, forgive us for doing as Sarah did, getting impatient when answers to our prayers seem so long in coming. Help us to remember that your ways, your timing, and your plans are always better than our own.

WEEK 3

HAGAR

"FLIGHT" OR "FLEEING" OR "STRANGER" OR "SOJOURNER"

Her Story

As a slave and a foreigner, Hagar was a pawn, subject to the whims of her master and mistress.

When [Hagar] knew she was pregnant, she began to despise her mistress. GENESIS 16:4

READ

Genesis 16; 21:8–21

Who WAS SHE?

Abraham left Egypt "with his wife and everything he had" (Genesis 13:1), including an Egyptian slave named Hagar, who was probably among the female servants Pharaoh gave Abraham in exchange for Sarah (Genesis 12:16). Perhaps more comely or more capable than other female slaves owned by Abraham, Hagar became Sarah's personal servant. Poor Hagar. She went from being a slave in Egypt, a piece of merchandise to be traded at Pharaoh's whim, to becoming the mother of Abraham's son, suffering abuse in the household of her master and mistress.

A *Closer Look* AT HAGAR'S STORY

HER STORY TOOK PLACE AROUND 2000–1800 BC.

In the world of the Bible, infertility was a personal and social catastrophe. If the wife could not bear children, the family would not survive. So central was this duty that some marriage contracts provided contingency plans in the event of barrenness. When Sarah suggested that Abraham sleep with her Egyptian maidservant, she may have been invoking the terms of her marriage contract.

Hagar's newly elevated status made her despise her mistress, with disastrous consequences, for Sarah felt her position in the household was being undermined. Hadn't she been sold into Pharaoh's harem during her sojourn in Egypt? What would prevent Abraham from setting her aside again, this time for a younger woman?

Instead of excusing Sarah's anxieties, the Bible includes the ugly truth that she treated Hagar harshly. So harshly, in fact, that Hagar fled to the surrounding wilderness, an arid and desolate region suitable only for snakes, scorpions, and wild goats. Wretched and alone, she suddenly heard an angel call her by name and instruct her to return to Sarah and submit to her. Then the angel delivered God's promise.

"You are now pregnant
  and you will give birth to a son.
You shall name him Ishmael,
  for the LORD has heard of your
    misery.
He will be a wild donkey of a man;
  his hand will be against everyone
  and everyone's hand against him,
and he will live in hostility
  toward all his brothers" (Genesis
    16:11-12).

Though Hagar had been abused and enslaved, her son would be free, for who can tame a wild donkey?

Hagar responded to this divine visitation by exclaiming, "You are the God who sees me . . . I have now seen the One who sees me" (Genesis 16:13). To see and to be seen—for every detail of her suffering to be noted and every plot point of her future to be foreseen—was comfort and hope enough for Hagar, who obeyed the Lord by returning home and submitting to Sarah. But why did she have to return? Perhaps because it was the only path to survival that she and her son, Ishmael, had at that time.

Several years later, when Sarah's miracle son, Isaac, was still a toddler, Sarah pleaded with Abraham to exile Hagar and Ishmael into the wilderness. After receiving a word from the Lord telling him to "listen to whatever Sarah tells you" (Genesis 21:12), Abraham sent Hagar and Ishmael into the wilderness.

But Hagar received a word from God too. Just as he had promised, God heard the boy's cries as he lay dying from thirst. He sent an angel to guide Hagar to a well that would nourish them. Then he reiterated his promise to make Ishmael into a great nation. As the story goes, "God was with the boy as he grew up" (Genesis 21:20). In the midst of weakness, brokenness, and sin, God furthered his plan while also caring for those who were ill-treated, abused, and shunned by the very people God had chosen for his own.

HAGAR'S *Legacy* IN SCRIPTURE

READ

Genesis 16

- Hagar had no control over her situation. As Sarah's servant/slave, she couldn't say no to their proposition. Have you ever been in a situation over which you had no control? How did you respond?

- Why did Hagar begin to despise Sarah? What do you think about Sarah's response?

- When God came to Hagar's rescue, he was the first one to call her by her name. She responded by giving him a name (Genesis 16:13). Have you ever felt like giving God a special name? What were the circumstances, and what name would you give to God?

- What can Hagar's story teach us about how to treat those who are mistreated in our world today?

READ

Genesis 21:8-21.

- For the second time, Hagar was in the wilderness. What is similar in the two stories? What is different? Compare also how Abraham reacted each time. What significant difference do you see?

- What does God's promise to Hagar in Genesis 21:18 reveal about his character? What assurance does this give you?

OUR *Connection* TO HAGAR

Despite her mistakes, Hagar discovered that God cared deeply about her and her child. He had seen her suffering, given her a way out, and then provided a legacy for her son, Ishmael, whose name means "God hears." How wonderful to know that God himself would always hear and respond to the cries of her child!

- Why do you think it was so important for Hagar to feel seen by God?

- Describe times in your life when you felt seen by others or by God. How has God communicated that he knows you and understands what you're facing?

- Reflect on how powerful God's promise was to Abraham—so powerful, in fact, that it spilled over into the life of a slave woman and her child. What does that say about the nature of God and the ways in which he interacts with us?

Father, thank you for revealing that you are the God who sees us just as you saw poor Hagar, and you will rescue us just as you rescued her. Thank you for being a God of such profound love and compassion.

WEEK 4

LOT'S WIFE

Her Story

Her fate was tragic—and memorable—perhaps because she was more attached to the good life than was good for her.

But Lot's wife looked back, and she became a pillar of salt. GENESIS 19:26

READ

Genesis 18:16–19:29; Luke 17:28–29

Who WAS SHE?

Lot's wife is notorious not for who she was but for what she became—a pillar of salt. Living in the city of Sodom must have felt more convenient than living in a tent near Hebron, as Lot's uncle Abraham did. Her hesitation when the angel twice urged her to "hurry" may reveal the depth to which Sodom's decadence had already entered her heart. Her attachments became all too evident when she ignored the angel's warning and turned back toward Sodom.

A *Closer Look* AT LOT'S WIFE'S STORY

HER STORY TOOK PLACE AROUND 2050–1950 BC.

Even people who have never cracked open a Bible recognize the name *Sodom* due to the city's scandalous reputation. The story of how a throng of men surrounded Lot's house in Sodom, demanding he surrender his guests to be gang-raped, is certainly not bedtime reading for small children. But what child wouldn't be captivated by the possibility of a woman turning into a pillar of salt?

Hospitality was considered a sacred duty in the world of the Bible. If people sat down at your table and were sheltered under your roof, you pledged to protect them, even at the cost of your life. Intent on shielding his guests from harm, Lot made a twisted decision to risk the rape and murder of his two virgin daughters by offering them as substitutes for his guests.

God had already revealed to Abraham his plan of coming judgment because of Sodom's widespread corruption. When the two angels urged Lot and his family to flee and not look back, it was the "not look back" part that further traumatized the family. Because Lot's wife did indeed look back and suffered the consequences as burning sulfur rained down upon the city, annihilating it and reducing her to a pillar of salt.

Perhaps it wasn't a mere glance back at the city to behold the spectacle of its terrible demise that was her fatal error. After all, the text says that the Lord didn't destroy the city until Lot and his two daughters reached the shelter of the nearby city of Zoar. But by then, his wife had already gone missing in action. Most likely she had not merely glanced back but actually turned back in order to reenter the city, thus sharing its fate.

Sin often has a certain stickiness to it. It can be hard to shake off. Even if we aren't doing something wrong, we may become comfortable with an atmosphere of sin. Perhaps we accommodate it by excusing actions we once knew to be wrong because they now seem so "normal." This may have been why Lot offered his daughters to the mob outside his house—and also why Lot's wife turned around. She had seen the corruption firsthand but preferred the city's comforts and her own way of life over following God's commands.

Jesus urged his followers to "Remember Lot's wife!" when speaking of his second coming (Luke 17:32). Unrepented sin eventually brings judgment. Our hearts can harden quickly or slowly, calcifying and turning to stone—or to salt, as in the case of Lot's wife. Her story warns us of the danger of resisting God's warnings, of turning back when he is urging us forward.

LOT'S WIFE'S *Legacy* IN SCRIPTURE

READ

Genesis 19:1-11

- What does Lot's response to the raiders tell you about the danger of becoming slowly conditioned to evil? How did life in Sodom skew his sense of right and wrong?

- Describe what you imagine Lot's wife thought of his proposition.

- What does this say about how ancient societies valued or devalued women?

READ

Genesis 19:15-26

- Why would Lot and his wife hesitate when the angel urged them to leave?

- Lot's wife couldn't resist looking back. What might have made her turn around to look? Do you think she was judged for a mere glance back or something more?

- How have you been tempted to look back, to hold on tightly to something or someone when God is telling you to let go?

- What might God be telling you through this story?

OUR *Connection* TO LOT'S WIFE

Sodom, which was located near the Dead Sea—the lowest place on earth—has come to symbolize a place of irredeemable corruption. Centuries later, the prophet Ezekiel had a vision of a river that would one day flow from the Jerusalem temple into the Dead Sea (Ezekiel 47:1–8), turning the salty, lifeless waters fresh. What a picture of how God's grace, in Jesus, can enliven even what seems hopelessly lost!

- The angels had meant to bless and protect Lot's wife, but she refused their guidance. How have God's warnings in Scripture or through others served to bless and protect you?

- Sometimes God says, "Enough and no more." Those times of judgment can lead to repentance and restoration. Or, as with Lot's wife, the judgment becomes final. If you sense that you've been ignoring a warning, simply ask God's forgiveness and then ask for grace to obey.

Lord, how easy it is for us to be like Lot's wife, hanging on to the past, mourning lost opportunities, yearning for ended relationships. Help us to let go, repent where it's needed, and move forward into a future you've planned, free from the past and its regrets.

WEEK 5

REBEKAH

"TO TIE" OR "TO BIND," ALSO INTERPRETED AS "CAPTIVATING"

Her Story

She tenderly comforted her new husband, Isaac, after the death of his mother. Later in life, she favored one son over the other, manipulating events as her mother-in-law Sarah had done years earlier.

Isaac . . . married Rebekah. So she became his wife, and he loved her; and Isaac was comforted after his mother's death. GENESIS 24:67

READ

Genesis 24; 25:19–34; 27:1–28:5

Who WAS SHE?

From a tender age, Rebekah showed great faith, choosing to leave home with a man she had just met to marry a man she had never met. Years later when she and Isaac played favorites with their twin sons, dysfunction and brokenness ensued. Her favorite son, Jacob, had to run for his life to escape the fury of his brother, Esau, and Rebekah never saw him again. Still, she was instrumental in helping to pass on the covenantal blessing within the family of God.

A Closer Look AT REBEKAH'S STORY

HER STORY TOOK PLACE AROUND 1900–1800 BC.

For the first twenty years of her marriage, Rebekah was probably ashamed of her barrenness because her world treated childlessness as a curse. At that time, people assumed God created babies when a man planted his seed into a woman's womb. They viewed women as incubators in which infants could grow. If a couple could not conceive or if a woman miscarried, she bore the blame.

Unlike her mother-in-law, Sarah, Rebekah's childlessness ended not by suggesting a surrogate pregnancy but after Isaac prayed for her. Blessed with twins, Rebekah's pregnancy brought its own share of troubles. Feeling a struggle within her womb, she prayed, asking God what was happening. His answer foreshadowed a long struggle with a final resolution.

> "Two nations are in your womb,
> and two peoples from within you will be separated;
> one people will be stronger than the other,
> and the older will serve the younger" (Genesis 25:23).

Years later, Isaac appeared in the story as an enfeebled old man who was conned by his younger son, Jacob. Aided and abetted by Rebekah, Jacob succeeded in stealing his brother Esau's blessing.

Philosopher and commentator Leon Kass makes the case that Rebekah should be praised, not criticized as she often is, for her scheme in favor of Jacob. Why? Because she helped Isaac do the right thing by passing on the covenantal blessing to Jacob, whom she recognized as the twin who was most likely to carry it forward.

According to Kass, Rebekah "acts with tact, delicacy and affection; though she arranges his deception, she does whatever she can to preserve and promote the dignity of her husband, whom she serves out of love. By the end, Rebekah's Isaac rises to the work of transmission and then becomes truly the son of Abraham. And Rebekah's Jacob, under the command first of his mother then his father, goes off to prepare himself to take his father's place as a link in the covenantal chain."

As evidence, Kass points out that instead of losing his temper when he discovered Jacob's deception, Isaac trembled in awe (Genesis 27:33). Maybe the old man recognized that a divine hand had just reached down and moved his own hand onto Jacob's head, thereby passing the covenantal blessing to his younger son.[3] Like other biblical heroes (e.g., Joseph, Moses, and David), Rebekah uses trickery to overcome a disadvantage and achieve an important purpose.

As you meditate on the story of this biblical matriarch who carried two nations within her womb, you may want to ask yourself which interpretation rings true. Was Rebekah a manipulative woman who merely wanted her favorite son to succeed (a view that only came into favor at the end of the nineteenth century)? Or was she a woman of destiny—a wise mother and wife whose main concern was to pass on the covenantal blessing to the proper son?

Rebekah's Jacob would later be renamed Israel, father to the twelve tribes of Israel (Genesis 32:28; 35:10). Her son Esau would become the father of the Edomites, one of whom was Herod the Great, who would do his murderous best to kill the infant Jesus (Matthew 2:16).

3 See Leon R. Kass, *The Beginning of Wisdom: Reading Genesis* (The University of Chicago Press, 2003), 376–403.

REBEKAH'S *Legacy* IN SCRIPTURE

READ

Genesis 24:10-27

What do young Rebekah's deeds reveal about her character?

READ

Genesis 24:50-67

- How does Rebekah respond when asked if she would go with Abraham's servant? What does her response tell you about her trust in God?

- When have you been asked to do something purely in faith? How did you respond?

- What words would you use to describe the early marriage relationship of Isaac and Rebekah?

READ

Genesis 25:21-28

- Why did Rebekah go to "inquire of the LORD" (v. 22)? Why was she concerned?

- How does God's answer play into her future actions?

- How does the sort of favoritism described in these verses affect family relationships? How have you been tempted to play favorites?

READ

Genesis 27:1-27

- After her earlier trust in God, why would Rebekah now use manipulation to get what God had promised?

- The entire story of Rebekah is rich and full of intrigue. In one sentence, summarize what you would like to learn from her life.

OUR *Connection* TO REBEKAH

The beautiful, strong-minded Rebekah was part of an extended family whose colorful story unfolds in the book of Genesis across four generations. Beginning with Abraham and threading its way to Joseph and the brothers who tried to kill him, it's a master class in the art of deception and family dysfunction. Yet it's the foundation story of the nation of Israel, God's chosen people.

- Genesis 24 tells how God chose Rebekah to become Isaac's wife. How might this story have shaped her actions, her sense of identity, and her destiny?

- When Rebekah felt trouble in her womb, she asked God for understanding. How might her experience of prayer, pregnancy, and the prophecy she received have affected her attitude?

What evidence might Rebekah have cited to support the view that Jacob was more fit than Esau to receive the covenant blessing and lead the clan?

Father, thank you for stories like Rebekah's. Her faltering steps remind me that you can also use my stumbles and awkward efforts to accomplish your purposes in my life and in the lives of those I love.

WEEK 6

RACHEL

"EWE," A FEMALE SHEEP

Her Story

Manipulated by her father, Rachel had little control over her own life circumstances. Finding it difficult to creatively deal with her situation, she behaved like a perpetual victim.

When Rachel saw that she was not bearing Jacob any children, she became jealous of her sister. So she said to Jacob, "Give me children, or I'll die!" GENESIS 30:1

READ

Genesis 29–35; Ruth 4:11; Jeremiah 31:15; Matthew 2:18

Who WAS SHE?

Rachel's father, Laban, a master of duplicity, substituted his older daughter, Leah, for his younger daughter, Rachel, on Jacob's wedding night. Though Jacob loved Rachel deeply, his love wasn't enough for her. While Leah had one son after another, Rachel remained childless. Desperate for children, Rachel finally had two sons through her maid Bilhah. Only later did she become pregnant herself with Joseph, who quickly became Jacob's favorite son. Tragically, on a journey with her family to Jacob's ancestral home, Rachel died while giving birth to Benjamin.

A Closer Look AT RACHEL'S STORY

HER STORY TOOK PLACE AROUND 1800–1700 BC.

"Oh, what a tangled web we weave when first we practice to deceive." This famous quote by Sir Walter Scott could have been written about many of our earliest spiritual ancestors. After Eve fell for the serpent's lie, several of her descendants became practiced in the art of deception. Here are just a few examples, drawn from the book of Genesis.

Abraham tricked Pharaoh into thinking Sarah was not his wife.

Rebekah urged her son Jacob to deceive his father, Isaac, in order to receive a blessing.

Rebekah's brother, Laban, tricked his nephew Jacob into marrying his cousin Leah and working for him for fourteen years.

Jacob deceived his father-in-law, Laban, into thinking he was not running away.

Rachel deceived her father when he tried to discover who had stolen his household idols.

Lies, deception, and trickery weave their way through the stories of many of the men and women we meet in the book of Genesis. In their attempt to control circumstances and gain favor, they failed to consider how their cleverness could create problems for themselves, unleashing consequences that would last for generations.

That was certainly the case when Laban switched Leah for Rachel in Jacob's marriage bed. After that, the sisters engaged in a nonstop competition for his favor, which was reflected even in the way they named their sons.

LEAH AND HER MAID ZILPAH'S SONS

Reuben—sounds like the Hebrew word for "he has seen my misery"

Simeon—"one who hears"

Levi—sounds like and may be derived from the Hebrew for "attached"

Judah—sounds like and may be derived from the Hebrew for "praise"

Gad—"a troop" or "good fortune"

Asher—"happy"

Issachar—sounds like the Hebrew for "reward"
Zebulun—"honor"

RACHEL AND HER MAID BILHAH'S SONS

Dan—"he has vindicated"
Naphtali—"my struggle"
Joseph—"may he add"
Benjamin—"son of my right hand"

Rachel's clever husband, Jacob, who had earlier deceived his father and stolen his brother Esau's blessing, was paid back amply, first at the hands of her father, Laban, and later by two of his own sons, who used deception to avenge the rape of their sister, Dinah. Still later, Jacob's sons tricked him into believing his favorite son, Joseph, had been mauled to death by a wild animal (Genesis 37:31-36). Even Joseph, Jacob's most cherished son, caused his father acute suffering by setting up a scheme to lure Jacob's youngest son, Benjamin, to Egypt (Genesis 42:18-43:14).

From the very beginning, a terrain of falsehoods would shape the journey of Rachel and her extended family—God's chosen but dysfunctional people—toward the fulfillment of God's promise to Abraham. The journey would be marked at times by joy and celebration, but more often by sorrow, struggle, and division.

RACHEL'S *Legacy* IN SCRIPTURE

READ

Genesis 29:15-30:24

Rachel and Leah may have been competitors even before they both married Jacob. How did their ability to have children affect their relationship after they married?

- Rachel expresses her agony over her childlessness in Genesis 30:1. How might Rachel's relationship with her sister, had it been healthy, have eased her pain? Do you know anyone in this kind of pain? What sort of encouragement might you offer them?

- In the beginning, Jacob's love was enough for Rachel. But then it gave way to discontent. How did that affect her relationship with her husband? How has discontentment affected your own life and relationships?

- List a few results of discontentment and then a few results of contentment.

READ

Genesis 35:16–20

- Compare these verses with Genesis 30:1. Rachel died giving birth to what she most wanted—another child. Was the price too high? What price would you be willing to pay for something you desperately want?

OUR *Connection* TO RACHEL

Imagine what Rachel must have felt when her father tricked her beloved Jacob into marrying her older sister, Leah. How unfair it must have seemed! Though first in her husband's affections, Rachel remained childless for many years. As the two sisters struggled with each other, their striving—and Jacob's favoritism—was passed on to their children with disastrous results (Genesis 37:1-28).

- If the Bible were mere propaganda, how likely is it that its earliest characters would be portrayed with so many flaws? How do Rachel's imperfections affect your appreciation for her story?

- Exodus 34:7 speaks about how God "punishes the children and their children for the sin of the parents to the third and fourth generation." How does this observation play out in the story? How has it played out in your extended family? How might God want to bring healing?

God of love and compassion, give us the honesty and insight it takes to recognize how nurturing our discontent will hurt us and those we love. Turn our hearts instead to you. Teach us the truth that only in you can we find true contentment.

WEEK 7

LEAH

HER NAME MAY MEAN "IMPATIENT" OR "WILD COW."

Her Story

Leah—the one who was not beautiful and not loved. Her one gift seemed to be an ability to bear children.

Leah had weak eyes, but Rachel . . . was beautiful . . . . [Jacob's] love for Rachel was greater than his love for Leah. GENESIS 29:17, 30

READ

Genesis 29–35; Ruth 4:11

Who WAS SHE?

Leah is best known not for what she had but for what she lacked—her husband's love. When God saw her pain, he blessed Leah with one child after another while Rachel remained childless and envious. Their mutual hurts generated a wrangling that went on for years, creating discord and misery for their entire household. Because Rachel died on a journey, Jacob buried her "beside the road" (Genesis 48:7). Leah, however, had the honor of being laid to rest next to Jacob in the family burial cave (Genesis 49:29–31).

A Closer Look AT LEAH'S STORY

HER STORY TOOK PLACE AROUND 1800–1700 BC.

Before God cast Eve out of paradise, he revealed a consequence that would thread its way through the lives of her descendants:

> "I will make your pains in childbearing very severe;
> with painful labor you will give birth to children.
> Your desire will be for your husband,
> and he will rule over you" (Genesis 3:16).

This age-old dynamic played out in the stories of Leah and her younger sister, Rachel, in particular ways. Unlike Rachel, Leah had little difficulty bearing children. Her trouble came when she tried to use them as currency to purchase what she longed for but never fully received—her husband's affection. Her desire was indeed for her husband, but Jacob ruled over her by playing favorites. Leah and Rachel's struggles and the resulting tension between their offspring were birthed by Jacob's favoritism, a trait passed down from his parents, Isaac and Rebekah (Genesis 25:27-28).

Leah would have been painfully aware of Jacob's shock and disappointment at discovering it was she and not Rachel in his marriage bed. But she wasn't at fault for her father's dishonesty. She was simply his daughter, duty bound to obey him.

With every child she would later bear, Leah's hope would rise: "Surely my husband will love me now" (Genesis 29:32). But Jacob had eyes only for Rachel. Fortunately, someone else had eyes for Leah. God had seen that she was unloved by the one she loved. During her difficult marriage, God gave her children.

Though blessed by God in ways that stirred Rachel's envy, Leah still felt the sting of being less loved. Nowhere was this more obvious than when Jacob arranged his children and their mothers in ascending order of value as he was about to face his estranged brother, Esau, and Esau's four hundred men. First, in the most vulnerable position, Jacob placed the concubines and their children, then Leah and her children, and then, at the very back—in the most protected place—he placed Rachel and her son Joseph. Observing this and what may have been additional slights against their mother and themselves, Jacob's older sons came to resent their father's favorite son, Joseph.

Though Jacob only had eyes for Rachel, God's eyes remained on Leah. Though Rachel's son Joseph would play a critical role in the preservation of the Hebrew people, the promised Savior would come through the line of Leah's son Judah, whose descendants would include King David and Jesus, the long-awaited Messiah.

LEAH'S *Legacy* IN SCRIPTURE

READ

Genesis 29:15-30

- What part might Leah have played in the wedding night deception? Victim? Participant?

READ

Genesis 29:31-30:21

- How do you think Leah might have felt toward Jacob and he toward her as the years passed? Read Genesis 29:31-34 to inform your answers.

- Have you ever felt unloved by someone? How did you respond?

- Note the names Leah gave to her first three sons. What do the names reveal about Leah and how she understood her worth? By contrast, what do the names Rachel gave to the sons born to Bilhah reveal about Rachel?

- Meditate for a while on the story of Leah. What one lesson might she have to teach you?

OUR *Connection* TO LEAH

Some of the Bible's most prominent men had polygamous marriages (e.g., Abraham, Jacob, Samson, David, and Solomon). Their stories display how this practice divided families and even threatened the nation. Leah and her sister, Rachel, had little agency in terms of entering into such a marriage. But they did have a choice in how they would respond to each other and to their respective children.

- How might Leah's life and the lives of her family have been different had she allowed herself to be deeply consoled by God's kindness?

- Take a few moments to consider how God has blessed you. How might those blessings bring you peace even in the midst of life's unfairness?

- God built his chosen people through two imperfect women—the only kind of women on the planet. Does that console or depress you? Why?

Father, your Word is an encouragement to me when I read the stories of these women and men. You made them part of your plan despite their imperfections. Use me too! I'm your servant in spite of my imperfections.

WEEK 8

TAMAR

"DATE TREE" OR "PALM TREE"

Her Story

Tamar sacrificed her dignity and virtue to gain what she had wanted all along: sons to continue the family line.

"She is more righteous than I, since I wouldn't give her to my son Shelah." GENESIS 38:26

READ

Genesis 38; Matthew 1:3

Who WAS SHE?

Driven by one overwhelming need, Tamar sacrificed her reputation and nearly her life. Her father-in-law, Judah, had wronged her by not giving his youngest son to be her husband, even though he had promised to do so. Disguised as a prostitute, she waited on the side of the road for only one customer, Judah. Though her act seems repugnant, it enabled the tribe of Judah, from which the Messiah would come, to continue. Tamar's story illustrates for us God's ability to work out his plans regardless of the circumstances.

A *Closer Look* AT TAMAR'S STORY

HER STORY TOOK PLACE AROUND 1715–1695 BC.

In the world Tamar inhabited, one of the worst things that could happen to a woman was becoming a childless widow. With neither sons nor a husband to provide for her, a widow would often lack the economic, legal, and social support to live.

Distasteful and puzzling as Tamar's story is for modern readers, it took place in a period when God's command in Genesis 1:28 to "be fruitful and increase in number" would have been an urgent necessity if the new nation were to survive. Jewish readers would have seen Tamar as a heroine rather than an immoral woman.

If a woman's husband died, it was her brother-in-law's duty to marry her. Since this practice was designed to perpetuate family continuity, the punishment for neglecting it was severe. God killed Onan, Judah's second son, for preventing Tamar from becoming pregnant. His motive? Any sons Tamar might have with him would diminish his own inheritance.

After Onan died, Judah promised Tamar to his youngest son. Fearing she might bestow the kiss of death on him, too, Judah failed to fulfill that promise when Shelah reached maturity. False though his promise was, it kept Tamar tethered to the family, preventing her from remarrying outside it, as she could have done had no suitable relative stepped up.

A sister-in-law/brother-in-law marriage would normally have been considered incestuous, but that designation was suspended with the death of Tamar's husband. The same was true for a daughter-in-law/father-in-law relationship. If a widow couldn't marry her brother-in-law, she was allowed to marry her father-in-law.

When, after their secret tryst, Tamar finally revealed that Judah had impregnated her, he was shocked into confessing the truth: "She is more righteous than I, since I wouldn't give her to my son Shelah" (Genesis 38:26).

Though Tamar must have felt all but forgotten by her family, she surely rejoiced when God remembered her by giving her twin sons. The eldest was Perez, from whose line would come Boaz, King David, and the wise King Solomon.

The book of Ruth depicts Tamar positively when, after Boaz declares his intention to marry Ruth, the elders say, "Through the offspring the LORD gives you by this young woman, may your family be like that of Perez, whom Tamar bore to Judah" (Ruth 4:12).

Matthew 1:1-16 lists Tamar among a handful of women in the genealogy of "Jesus the Messiah." The stories of these women are laced with distasteful details like incest, out-of-wedlock pregnancies, and even murder. Still, each woman is remembered as part of a vital chain of broken human beings that stretches from Abraham to Joseph, the husband of Mary, the mother of Jesus, who is called the Christ. As the Scripture says, "Many are the plans in a person's heart, but it is the LORD's purpose that prevails" (Proverbs 19:21).

Tamar's *Legacy* in Scripture

READ

Genesis 38; Matthew 1:3

- None of the men in Tamar's life fulfilled their responsibility to her, including her father-in-law, Judah. How did the inaction of these men put Tamar in an intolerable situation?

- Why was Tamar desperate to have a child?

- Consider Judah's statement in Genesis 38:26. Why would he say this? What does this reveal about the power of truth-telling?

- What is the significance of Tamar, who was likely a Gentile, being mentioned in the family line of Jesus? What does this say about who God is and who he chooses to use for his eternal purposes?

OUR *Connection* TO TAMAR

Tamar lived in an honor-and-shame culture in which female members had few rights. Though she had been wronged by Judah's two sons and then by Judah himself, she didn't simply resign herself to their treatment. Instead, she acted boldly, creatively, and independently, resulting in Judah's eyes being opened to the injustice he and his sons had perpetrated on her. Though living in a culture vastly different from our own, Tamar showed that agency and courage could help turn a situation around.

- Judah seems more foolish than evil in this story. What does this reveal about how people who possess power but lack understanding can turn into oppressors?[4]

- What does Tamar's story tell us about God's ability to redeem evil even in the midst of entrenched family dysfunction?

---

4 See Tikva Frymer-Kensky, *Reading the Women of the Bible* (Schocken Books, 2002), 267; 273–274.

God of grace and goodness, thank you for how often you used women in the Bible to turn men away from infidelity or a disastrous course of action. Thank you for their examples of faithfulness and perseverance in the middle of great difficulty.

WEEK 9

POTIPHAR'S WIFE

Her Story

The wife of a prosperous and influential Egyptian, she proved unfaithful and vindictive, ready to lie to protect herself and ruin an innocent man.

Now Joseph was well-built and handsome, and after a while his master's wife took notice of Joseph. GENESIS 39:6-7

READ

Genesis 39

Who WAS SHE?

Potiphar's wife had only one thing on her mind—how to seduce the well-built, handsome slave her husband had put in charge of their household. Day after day she harassed him, and day after day Joseph refused to go to bed with her. Finally, she took revenge, accusing Joseph of attempted rape. Her accusation forced her husband, Potiphar, to respond by putting Joseph in prison.

A Closer Look AT POTIPHAR'S WIFE'S STORY

HER STORY TOOK PLACE AROUND 1715–1705 BC.

Like his great-grandparents Abraham and Sarah, Rachel's son Joseph went down to Egypt, but not willingly and not to escape a famine. This idea of "going down" to Egypt, which appears in many places in the Bible, has both geographical and metaphorical meaning. Joseph "went down" both by traveling south from Canaan to Egypt and by descending into a culture that knew nothing of God. Indeed, he would both shape and be shaped by an empire that would enslave his people for four hundred years (Genesis 15:12-14).

Stripped of his ornate coat by brothers who hated him, Joseph had been thrown into a pit and later sold to Ishmaelite traders, who then arranged for his enslavement in Egypt. In a sad twist, these men—descendants of Abraham through Hagar the Egyptian—would have been Joseph's second or third cousins.

When Joseph arrived in Egypt, Potiphar, Pharaoh's captain of the guard, purchased him. Because God was with Joseph, everything he did succeeded, which made him the favorite of his master. Unfortunately for Joseph, his good looks also made him the favorite of Potiphar's wayward wife.

Though Scripture never mentions her name, she is the picture of the adulteress that the book of Proverbs later warns against (Proverbs 7:15-19). As such, she is one of only a handful of female characters in Scripture without any redeeming qualities. By falsely accusing Joseph of attempted rape and repeatedly stressing his lowly status as both a slave and a foreigner to gain sympathy for her accusations, she abused her own position of power and privilege.

Though his wife's accusations upset Potiphar, the Bible doesn't say where he directed his anger. Perhaps he suspected his wife of lying and resented her for depriving him of his most valuable slave. That would explain why he merely imprisoned Joseph rather than executed him, as would more commonly have been the case. Furthermore, as captain of the guard, he confined Joseph to the special prison that housed Pharaoh's prisoners, the very ones who would provide the means for Joseph to later be set free and then elevated to a position of power in Egypt.

Twice in his life, Joseph had been stripped of everything he had, first by his brothers who tore off his beautiful coat and threw him into a pit and second by a woman who tore off his cloak as he fled and then had him thrown into prison. But no pit or prison could keep hold of a man whom God was determined to bless.

Thousands of years later, the apostle Paul would encourage Roman Christians, who would soon undergo persecution, with words Joseph would surely have approved, and which we can claim as our own today: "If God is for us, who can be against us?" (Romans 8:31).

Potiphar's Wife's *Legacy* in Scripture

READ
Genesis 39:1-20

- Why would a woman with such wealth and privilege desire poor, marginalized Joseph?

- What do her actions reveal about her character?

- Where did Joseph's strength of character to resist this seduction come from?

- If you have sin or rejection in your own past or in your own family, explore how it has affected you. Has it produced strength or weakness?

- Everyone faces temptation. Even Jesus was tempted! What sort of temptations are common for you personally and for today's culture? How do you deal with temptation? For help, consult 1 Corinthians 10:12-13.

OUR *Connection* TO POTIPHAR'S WIFE

Like Eve, who saw that the fruit of the tree of the knowledge of good and evil was "pleasing to the eye" (Genesis 3:6), Potiphar's wife saw that Joseph was beautiful to look at. She reached for him just as Eve had reached for the forbidden fruit. In the kind of irony that only God can achieve, she became the instrument not for Joseph's demise but for his eventual elevation to a place of greatness (see Genesis 40-41).

- How does our desire for beautiful people and things tempt us to redefine good and evil as Eve and Potiphar's wife did? What can help us resist this inclination?

- Potiphar's wife called attention to Joseph's status as a slave and foreigner, marking him as "other." How does this tendency manifest itself today? Have you ever been made to feel "other"? If so, how did you deal with it?

Father God, this story reminds us of two things—the danger of yielding to temptation but also the goodness of knowing that you watch over us. You give us grace to resist when we need to, and you also bring goodness out of things intended to harm us.

WEEK 10

THE MOTHERS OF MOSES

JOCHEBED

"YAHWEH IS GLORY"

Her Story

She acted boldly and cleverly in a time of slavery to save the son she loved.

When she saw that he was a fine child, she hid him for three months. EXODUS 2:2

PHARAOH'S DAUGHTER

Her Story

She acted boldly and with compassion to save the life of a Hebrew baby who had been born into slavery.

She saw the basket among the reeds . . . . She opened it and saw the baby. He was crying, and she felt sorry for him. EXODUS 2:5-6

READ
Exodus 2:1-10

Who WERE THEY?

Two mothers—one a slave, one a princess. Both would shape the child with their love and compassion. Jochebed put her baby into the Nile River just as Pharaoh had ordered, but on her terms. How she must have rejoiced when Pharaoh's daughter rescued him! Feeling sorry for the little one, Pharaoh's daughter scooped him out of the water and saved his life. Then she adopted him, bringing him up with all the privilege and education of a prince in Pharaoh's household.

A *Closer Look* AT THE MOTHERS OF MOSES' STORY

THEIR STORIES TOOK PLACE AROUND 1350 BC.

Nearly four hundred years after the story of Potiphar's wife came two remarkable women at the opposite ends of the spectrum of privilege and power. One was a slave named Jochebed, while the other was the daughter of a powerful pharaoh who was trying to wipe out every male baby of his Hebrew slaves. Politically, financially, ethnically, and spiritually, these two women couldn't have been more different. Yet God used both of them to save the life of the little boy who would one day become Israel's deliverer.

In one of the Bible's great ironies, of which there are many, God planted this future deliverer in the midst of Pharaoh's household. How like the Almighty to play his opening gambit by choosing the weak things of this world to overturn the powerful! For who in the ancient world was weaker than women and children, even if one of the women was an Egyptian princess?

The Lord must have been watching closely as Jochebed nestled her baby boy into a tar-covered basket and then surrendered him to the Nile River. He would have looked on as Pharaoh's daughter plucked Moses out of the water, rescuing him from the crocodiles and cobras sunning themselves on the riverbanks. Perhaps he chuckled when she offered to pay Jochebed to nurse her own baby. He may have snorted with laughter as he watched Moses grow up right under Pharaoh's nose.

Who was this murderous Pharaoh who became a symbol of satanic power in the epic battle that took place in Exodus? There were two kings of Egypt who played this role. The first ruled when Moses was born and was growing up in the palace. The second came to power after Moses had fled into the desert and later returned to Egypt. Scholars are uncertain of their identities.

Both would have ruled as gods among their people. Their great power derived in part from the life-giving Nile River, which flooded at regular intervals, depositing rich soil in which abundant crops grew. Oddly, it was Rachel's son Joseph who, hundreds of years earlier, had lifted the kings of Egypt high above their subjects. He did it by filling Pharaoh's storehouses with grain during seven years of plenty in advance of seven years of famine (Genesis 41:41–57). Year after year people paid dearly to keep themselves alive, which is how so much wealth and land migrated to Pharaoh's coffers.

Despite their eventual enslavement, Joseph's descendants kept multiplying. Fearing a slave revolt, Pharaoh tried to reduce their numbers by ordering every male baby to be thrown into the Nile River. How strange, since the Egyptians revered the river as the source of life. But it was out of that very river that the Lord plucked the little boy Moses, preserving his life through the wise, loving, and courageous acts of his biological and adoptive mothers so that his chosen people could one day go free.

THE MOTHERS OF MOSES' *Legacy* IN SCRIPTURE

READ

Exodus 2:1–4

- Name some of Jochebed's character traits based on her actions in these verses.

- Why would she have acted at this three-month point in her baby's life?

- What might Jochebed's goal have been? What might she have been hoping for?

READ
Exodus 2:5-10

- Name some of Pharaoh's daughter's character traits based on her actions in these verses.

- When the boy was weaned, Pharaoh's daughter named him Moses and said, "I drew him out of the water" (verse 10). How does this statement express her act of defiant resistance?

READ
Hebrews 11:23

- What does this verse say about the actions of Moses' parents?

- If you are a mother, have you ever been in a dire situation with one of your children? Where did you find the faith to act? How did you choose between fear and faith? If you don't have children, have you ever acted out of faith on behalf of someone else despite the fear you felt?

OUR *Connection* TO THE MOTHERS OF MOSES

The Hebrew word used for Moses' basket is *tevah*, the same word used for the ark that Noah built (Genesis 6–9). This word appears nowhere else in the Bible. Just as God saved humanity by instructing Noah to build an ark, God used Jochebed to craft a little ark that would save Moses, who would later deliver God's chosen people.

- Though the Lord heard the slaves' cries for deliverance (Exodus 2:23–24), it took years for Moses to grow up and become their leader. How might this story increase your confidence that even now God may be preparing an answer to your prayers?

- Pharaoh made the mistake of discounting the women, underestimating the danger they represented to his kingdom. How does God overturn human notions of power to defeat his enemies? What might have happened had Jochebed or Pharaoh's daughter been too timid to save a child?

- How has the Lord asked you to take risks as you follow him? Is there anything he is asking of you right now?

Lord, thank you for always orchestrating our lives' events to glorify you. Remind us often, through your Word and your presence, that you are with us and that your plan for us is better than any we could devise on our own.

WEEK 11

MIRIAM

HER NAME MAY MEAN "BITTERNESS" OR "BELOVED."

Her Story

She led a dance of joy and celebration after the Israelites crossed the Red Sea on dry ground and the waters crashed over the Egyptian army.

Miriam the prophet . . . took a timbrel in her hand, and all the women followed her, with timbrels and dancing. EXODUS 15:20

READ

Exodus 2:1-10; 14:1-15:21; Numbers 12:1-15

Who WAS SHE?

A sister, dancer, prophet, and leader, Miriam appears in scenes along with Moses—when he was her baby brother, when he led the Israelites out of Egypt, when she rebelled against his leadership and was punished for it, and when she finally died during the drawn-out and difficult journey to Canaan. She lived a long and eventful life, part of the leadership trio God had put together from one family: two brothers and their sister—Moses, Aaron, and Miriam.

A *Closer Look* AT MIRIAM'S STORY

HER STORY TOOK PLACE SOMEWHERE AROUND 1300–1200 BC.

Miriam grew up in the Nile River Delta, on fertile land that her ancestor Joseph (Jacob and Rachel's son) had secured for his family when they first settled in Egypt (Genesis 45:10-11). By the time Miriam and her brothers were born, Jacob's descendants had long been enslaved.

Most of us have heard the dramatic story of the exodus, when God liberated the Israelites from their Egyptian overlords. Movies like *The Ten Commandments* and *The Prince of Egypt* depicted thousands of Hebrew slaves engaged in the backbreaking labor of erecting royal tombs. But by the time Jacob's family settled in Egypt, pyramid building had gone out of style. Even so, the Hebrew slaves were engaged in cruel labor, forced to build huge storage cities for Pharaoh.

Like her mother Jochebed, Miriam seems anything but passive. After she saw Pharaoh's daughter rescue Moses from the Nile River, she boldly approached the Egyptian princess with a clever question: "Shall I go and get one of the Hebrew women to nurse the baby for you?" When the answer was yes, she recruited her mother for the job. Not only was Jochebed able to care for her son for the first two to three years of his life, but she also got paid for it!

Interesting that five females—Jochebed, Pharaoh's daughter, Miriam, and two midwives, Shiphrah and Puah (Exodus 1:15-22), whose names mean "beautiful" and "sparkle"—were the ones who scuttled Pharaoh's genocidal plan and inaugurated the events that led to the exodus. No doubt he had missed the possibility that mere women might pose a threat to his power.

Miriam lived with her little brother until he was weaned. Perhaps she told Moses stories about his Hebrew heritage, about the one God they worshiped in contrast to the hundreds of gods revered by the Egyptians. Later, Moses moved to the home of his adoptive mother, where he lived as an Egyptian.

Whether Miriam had any contact with Moses after he moved to the palace, the Bible doesn't say. But years later, at the age of forty, Moses fled Egypt, escaping to the wilderness after killing an Egyptian who had beaten a Hebrew slave. It would take an additional forty years of desert-shaping experiences before he would become the kind of deliverer God wanted him to be.

Moses was eighty the next time Miriam saw him, and she even older! As the journey out of Egypt and through the desert grew long and hard, God punished her for joining her brother Aaron in challenging Moses' leadership. The two had endangered the unity of God's people by opposing their brother, whose leadership was crucial to their survival. Strong and brave though she was, Miriam suffered a punishment designed to bring her to repentance. The last we hear of her is when she is buried in Kadesh Barnea, not far from where Hagar, another slave woman, had encountered an angel many years earlier (Genesis 16:7-10, 13-14).

Like her brothers Aaron and Moses, Miriam died before the Israelites crossed into the promised land. Like them, she became one of the great heroes of our faith. As a prophet, she exhorted and encouraged God's people and led them in a victory celebration after Pharaoh and his men drowned in the Red Sea.

MIRIAM'S *Legacy* IN SCRIPTURE

READ

Exodus 15:19-21

- Describe what you think it would have been like to walk through the Red Sea with the Egyptian army bearing down on you. Now describe what the women might have felt when they reached the other side and saw the waters crash down over the Egyptian army. Why was dancing their response? Whom did they praise?

- When have you experienced incredible joy or deliverance? How did you respond?

READ
Number 12:1-15

- How did Miriam undermine Moses' leadership? What might her actions have produced had God not reprimanded her? What other, underlying issues might Miriam have had with Moses other than the woman he had taken as wife?

- Using available study Bibles, commentaries, or the Internet, try to discover why God's punishment fell on Miriam but not on Aaron.

- How can we know that Aaron recognized his part in the rebellion?

- What does Numbers 12:13 tell us about Moses?

- How has God shown you mercy, even when you sin?

OUR *Connection* TO MIRIAM

The high drama of Exodus shapes both Jews and Christians, who understand that each of us is meant to identify personally with the story. Just as the Israelites were in bondage to an evil ruler, we are beset by evils from which only God can deliver us. If we follow him, he will lead us out of bondage and into a life of freedom.

- What adjectives would you use to describe Miriam? In what ways are you similar and dissimilar?

- Miriam would have had her own desert-shaping experience when she left Egypt. Describe such an experience in your own life and how it has affected your response to God.

- Miriam is an inspiration for every Christian, male or female. Reflect on how her example might have special significance for anyone who has ever been oppressed and abused or whose ancestors have been enslaved.

Lord, thank you for spiritual ancestors like Miriam, strong women who followed you closely and were willing to be used in your plan. Thank you for revealing not only their righteousness but also their brokenness, so that we can recognize you are able to use us too, broken as we are.

WEEK 12

RAHAB

HER NAME MAY MEAN "STORM" OR "ARROGANCE" OR "BROAD" OR "SPACIOUS."

Her Story

She bravely protected Hebrew spies and gained a place in the lineage of Jesus Christ.

"Now then, please swear to me by the LORD that you will show kindness to my family, because I have shown kindness to you." JOSHUA 2:12

READ

Joshua 2-3; 6:1-25

Who WAS SHE?

Rahab harbored two Israelite spies when fear permeated Jericho because of the rumored success of the Israelite army. Recognizing that her city would become their next casualty, she hid the spies from the king of Jericho, when they promised, "Our lives for yours." Her courage saved her family and forged a way for Joshua and his people to enter the land God had promised. She is mentioned in the ancestry of both King David and Jesus Christ.

A *Closer Look* AT RAHAB'S STORY

HER STORY TOOK PLACE AROUND 1220–1210 BC.

Just as key female figures sparked the exodus from Egypt, a woman helped the Israelites enter the promised land after their forty-year journey in the desert. A Canaanite, Rahab lived in Jericho, a fortified city located along important trade routes just fifteen miles from Jerusalem. Its existence dates to the ninth millennium BC, which places it among the oldest urban sites in history.

Since innkeepers were often associated with prostitution, the term for *prostitute* may also have meant "innkeeper." Tucked inside the city walls, Rahab's house was an excellent place to host travelers from all over the region carrying news of the world beyond. She would have listened to stories about the horde of Israelites who had encamped just east of the Jordan River, some fifteen miles away.

Rahab also would have heard how the Israelites left Egypt in triumph, and how their God reached down and parted the waters so they could walk across the sea to freedom. Forty years in the wilderness had toughened them, making them into a formidable fighting force. She also knew that the flooded Jordan River was impossible for such a large group of people to cross in springtime. But what would happen once the river dried up? That was the terrifying question on everyone's mind.

The Code of Hammurabi (laws in Mesopotamia that date back to about 1772 BC) prescribed the death penalty for any woman innkeeper who failed to report criminals. Rahab knew the mortal risk of harboring the Israelite spies.

What she didn't know was that as soon as the spies returned to Joshua with their encouraging report, he ordered the priests to carry the ark of the covenant into the flooded Jordan River so the people could cross. Had she known, she might have imagined what this "crossing over" would mean to those who had left Egypt when they were only children. They knew God had opened a path through the Red Sea while they and their parents and grandparents fled from Pharaoh. Now they were crossing another river, only this time they were the advancing army marching into the land God had promised.

The Bible says that "the water from upstream stopped flowing. It piled up in a heap a great distance away, at a town called Adam" (Joshua 3:16). Perhaps an earthquake caused the high banks of the Jordan to collapse upstream from where the Israelites were crossing, damming up the river. The walls of Jericho may have collapsed because of a second earthquake, which enabled Joshua and his men to breach the city's defenses. Such a theory doesn't diminish the miraculous aspects of the story but only points to God's power as the Lord of creation.

Because of Rahab's courage in aiding the Israelite spies, only she and her family survived. Leaving the devastated city behind, they settled with the Israelites. One of her descendants was King David. To later generations, she became known as the great-great-great-beyond-counting grandmother of Jesus Christ.

RAHAB'S *Legacy* IN SCRIPTURE

READ

Joshua 2:1–21

- Why would Rahab betray her own people and help the Israelite spies?

- What do you think about Rahab's lies to the king's men? When, if ever, is it okay to lie?

- What was the purpose of the scarlet cord in Joshua 2:18? Does it hold any special significance?

- What reaction do you have to God's use of a known prostitute to protect his people?

READ

James 2:25-26

- James commends Rahab, linking her budding faith in God to her actions. Where do you see Rahab's faith in action in Joshua?

- What are some real-life ways you can demonstrate your faith by your actions?

OUR *Connection* TO RAHAB

How could Rahab's house have survived an earthquake? Early twentieth century excavations have revealed a portion of the lower city wall of Jericho that did not collapse. Houses that were built against it were still intact.

- Rahab's story is a little like the story of Noah and his family, who were saved from destruction during a time of judgment. Instead of a boat, God used a house as a place of refuge. Genesis 6:9 says that "Noah was a righteous man, blameless among the people of his time." But Rahab doesn't seem to fit this description. What does her story reveal about how God sees and rewards people?

- Compare Exodus 12:7, 22–23 with Joshua 2:17–21. Reflect on the connection between these two stories as well as how they might foreshadow the saving work Jesus accomplished on the cross.

Father, our righteous God, worthy of all our praise, we thank you for people like Rahab who were willing to risk everything for your sake and your plans. Give us that kind of courage, Lord, so that you can use us to advance your plans.

WEEK 13

DEBORAH

"HONEY BEE"

Her Story

She listened to God and stepped outside cultural norms to lead the Israelites to victory in battle.

Now Deborah, a prophet, the wife of Lappidoth, was leading Israel at that time. JUDGES 4:4

READ

Judges 4-5

Who WAS SHE?

Jews and Christians alike celebrate Deborah for her skills and bravery. When God called, she took on a role usually reserved for men. Instead of fearing a battle with Sisera, Deborah stepped out courageously, fully trusting in God's deliverance. In her many roles—leader, judge, prophet, wife, mother—Deborah remained faithful to the God who guided her. As a result, Israel knew freedom from oppression for forty years.

A *Closer Look* AT DEBORAH'S STORY

HER STORY TOOK PLACE SOMEWHERE AROUND 1200–1100 BC.

After Rahab survived the spectacular collapse of Jericho's walls, Moses' successor, Joshua, began to subdue Canaan. But after Joshua's death, the people began to lose their way. New generations quickly forgot the wonderful things God had done and began worshiping Canaanite gods. When God withdrew his hand of blessing, one terrible defeat followed another until the people fell under the thumb of foreign oppressors once more.

Over and over, the pattern repeated itself. Disobedience eventually resulted in a flood of defeat. In their pain, the people would cry out to God, and he would raise up a deliverer in the form of a ruler, called a "judge." These were not kings but charismatic leaders who were often military leaders as well. In addition to Deborah, famous judges included Gideon, Samson, and the prophet Samuel.

Though leadership offices were usually barred to women, the role of prophet—someone who heard and spoke messages from God—was open to them. By Deborah's time, Jabin, king of Canaan, had been cruelly oppressing the Israelites for twenty years. His general, Sisera, commanded nine hundred chariots fitted with iron, an enormous technological advantage. With the odds so obviously favoring him, Sisera never suspected that God was about to use Deborah like another Moses to deliver his people.

Like Moses, Deborah was a prophet who arbitrated disputes. Just as people did in Moses' day, Deborah's people cried out for deliverance. As Moses had faced down Pharaoh's chariots at the Red Sea, she and Barak faced down an army of chariots surrounding Mount Tabor. Like Moses, Deborah supervised the battle from a distance. And like him, her career spanned forty years.

For his part, Sisera was like a mini pharaoh. Much like the Egyptians who tried to trap the Israelites at the edge of the sea, Sisera thought he had trapped the Israelite troops gathered on Mount Tabor. But then torrents of rain began pouring from heaven, flooding the Kishon River and miring Sisera's nine hundred chariots and horses in mud. That made his army sitting ducks for the onrushing Israelites as they swept down from Mount Tabor and crushed them. Once again, God had marshaled the forces of nature to enable his people to defeat what seemed an invincible enemy.

Moses had sung a song of victory with the Israelites at the edge of the Red Sea, celebrating God's amazing deliverance. Deborah and her commander, Barak, also sang, and this was their song:

> "When the princes in Israel take the lead,
> when the people willingly offer
> themselves—
> praise the LORD!
> Hear this, you kings! Listen, you rulers!
> I, even I, will sing to the LORD . . . .
> Villagers in Israel would not fight;
> they held back until I, Deborah, arose,
> until I arose, a mother in Israel . . .
> The river Kishon swept them away,
> the age-old river, the river Kishon.
> March on, my soul; be strong!
> Then thundered the horses' hooves—
> galloping, galloping go his mighty
> steeds" (Judges 5:2-3, 7, 21-22).

Like an ancient Joan of Arc, Deborah, Israel's fourth judge, rallied her people, leading them back to God and to a victory that produced peace for the next forty years.

DEBORAH'S *Legacy* IN SCRIPTURE

READ

Judges 4:1-10; 5:7

- What four roles of Deborah can be found in Judges 4:4-5—one personal and three national?

- As you read the story, what kind of leadership skills do you see in Deborah?

- Why did Barak want Deborah to go with him into battle?

- What, according to Deborah, will be the result if she accompanies Barak? Why is this significant?

- What does Judges 5:21 reveal are the consequences of the rain mentioned in verse 4?

- What character traits of Deborah would you most like to possess?

OUR *Connection* TO DEBORAH

Like a mother bear, Deborah arose, a "mother in Israel," to protect her cubs (Judges 5:7). She delivered the children of Israel by believing God, speaking his word, leading courageously, and offering wise counsel.

- Barak told Deborah, "If you go with me, I will go; but if you don't go with me, I won't go" (Judges 4:8). Compare this with Moses' statement to the Lord in Exodus 33:15. How have you responded when God has asked you to do something you didn't want to do?

- Throughout Judges, we see a stupid cycle of repeated disobedience leading to repeated defeats. How has this "stupid cycle" played out in your own life, and how might God want to deliver you from it?

- Think about the victories God has already achieved in your life and consider writing a song or poem to commemorate them.

Lord, you are not only a God of justice but also a God of mercy. When I disobey your commands or turn from you, please don't abandon me to my foolishness. Search me, find me, and in your love and grace, redeem me.

WEEK 14

JAEL

"A WILD OR MOUNTAIN GOAT"

Her Story

She used the simple tools she had on hand, as well as her wit and courage, to defeat a powerful enemy.

Jael went out to meet Sisera and said to him, "Come, my lord, come right in. Don't be afraid." JUDGES 4:18

READ

Judges 4-5

Who WAS SHE?

Jael was alone when danger and opportunity arrived. Sisera, a Canaanite general running for his life after being defeated by Deborah, Barak, and the Israelite forces, approached her tent. Would she help or obstruct him? She made a surprising choice since her husband had a peace treaty with the Canaanite king who employed Sisera. Relying only on her wits and a couple of household items, in an act both brave and gruesome, she delivered the decisive blow that made her a hero in the eyes of the Israelites. Deborah's song of praise after their victory includes an ode to Jael's courage.

A *Closer Look* AT JAEL'S STORY

HER STORY TOOK PLACE SOMEWHERE AROUND 1200–1100 BC.

Jael's husband, Heber, was part of Moses' father-in-law's family. They were Kenites, not Hebrews. Heber had made a peace treaty with the Canaanite king of Hazor, whose commander was Sisera, general of the army intent on eviscerating Israel. Since Kenites were often smiths, Heber may have pitched his tent near the battle to provide support for Sisera's weaponry.[5]

When Barak and his army swooped down from Mount Tabor, only one man escaped, and that man was Sisera. The once powerful general took off running. He must have thought himself lucky when he encountered Jael, who welcomed him like his own mother might have, offering him refuge inside her tent, a drink to rebuild his strength, and a blanket under which he could rest. Then, while he slept, she picked up a tent peg and drove it through his skull.

What an ironic ending to the story of a strong man whose power to terrify had rested on the advanced weaponry he possessed! Israel's army had stripped Sisera of everything that had made him look strong. Then a woman used a low-tech weapon—a wooden hammer and a peg that had been lying around her home—to slay him.

Barbaric as Jael's actions seem to modern readers, Deborah hailed her as a blessed woman, as indeed she would have been to the Israelites. Her victory came by breaking every social norm that stood in her way. She violated her husband's right to offer hospitality to other men; she broke the covenant her husband had made with the Canaanite king; and she pretended to offer Sisera safe hospitality—a sacred duty in her world—in order to slay him.[6]

---

5 Frymer-Kensky, *Reading the Women of the Bible*, 53.

6 See note on Judges 4:18–21, *NIV Cultural Backgrounds Study Bible*, ed. John H. Walton and Craig S. Keener (Zondervan, 2016), 416.

Jael's remarkable triumph would have shamed both generals in the story—the dead Sisera and the living Barak, who arrived on the scene too late to destroy his enemy. Just as Deborah had foretold, the honor of killing Sisera would go not to Barak but to a nomadic female by the name of Jael.

Deborah's victory song pictured Sisera's mother at home awaiting her son's victorious return. Surely he would bring plunder with him, she mused. A girl or even two girls for each man! Little did she know that two girls had already finished him off.[7]

7 Frymer-Kensky, *Reading the Women of the Bible*, 52.

JAEL'S *Legacy* IN SCRIPTURE

READ

Judges 4:16–22; 5:6, 24–27

- Jael's husband, Heber, had an alliance with King Jabin, the very king who had sent Sisera to defeat the Israelites. Why would Jael kill someone who was an ally of her husband?

- What about Jael made her the woman for this job? Review the meaning of her name, and discuss how she lived up to it.

- Use Deborah's words in Judges 5 to describe Jael. How does this differ from your impressions of Jael from Judges 4 and the actual events?

- What does this story tell you about who God will use to accomplish his purposes?

- What else can God possibly teach you from the story of Jael and her brutal deeds?

OUR *Connection* TO JAEL

Though the story never discloses Jael's motives for acting as she does, surely God was making a point. Israel had been weakened because of its disobedience. But God was still strong and still faithful. His deliverance could come from any direction he chose, no matter how improbable. Like Rahab, Jael was a non-Israelite who acted independently and courageously on behalf of a people not her own.

- The Bible speaks about God sitting in heaven and laughing at his enemies (Psalm 2:4). Gruesome as Jael's story is, how might it confirm that picture of God's attitude toward every obstacle and enemy?

- Take a moment to think about your deepest struggles, and then ask God for an image of the victory he wants to give you. Picture him laughing as he considers how he will defeat the devil and help you overcome.

Lord, thank you for using the weak to defeat the strong when the strong are in opposition to you. Help me in every situation to be attuned to you, to be willing and able to do whatever it takes to bring you glory and further your kingdom.

WEEK 15

DELILAH

HER NAME MAY MEAN "WEAK," "DAINTY ONE," OR "DARK ONE."

Her Story

She used her wiles to badger and then cut off the hair of God's strongman, rendering him weak and harmless.

With such nagging she prodded him day after day until he was sick to death of it. So he told her everything. JUDGES 16:16-17

READ
Judges 16

Who WAS SHE?

The strongman Samson was Israel's worst judge, and Delilah was his lover. Tragically, she loved money more than she cared for him. Philistine rulers offered her an enormous sum to discover the secret of his great strength. Though Samson tried to outlast her, Delilah kept pestering him until he told her the truth. His strength vanished as soon as his hair was cut off. Blinded and enslaved by his captors, Israel's hero seemed defeated. But what neither Delilah nor the Philistines suspected was that even though Samson was morally and physically weak, the God he served was strong.

A *Closer Look* AT DELILAH'S STORY

HER STORY TOOK PLACE AROUND 1100 BC.

A rolling avalanche of a man, Samson simply crushed his enemies, the Philistines, whenever they crossed him. Delilah's boyfriend Samson, one of Israel's judges, was a primary example of the tendency at that time for "everyone [to do] as they saw fit" (Judges 17:6; 21:25). Samson's supernatural strength couldn't make up for his many moral failures. Despite his many flaws, he ruled for twenty years, half the length that Deborah had ruled.

Though Samson fell in love with Delilah, nowhere in the story do we hear that Delilah loved Samson. Some have noted that her name sounds like *layla*, the Hebrew word for "night." She is like the woman in Proverbs who said, "Come, let's drink deeply of love till morning; let's enjoy ourselves with love! ... Many are the victims she has brought down; her slain are a mighty throng" (Proverbs 7:18, 26).

Curiously, Delilah seems to be an independent woman, a rarity in that day and age. Even the prostitute Rahab had family members whose safety concerned her (Joshua 2:12–13). But Delilah's identity isn't linked to being anyone's daughter, sister, wife, or mother. Acting independently, she does whatever she pleases. As such, she comes across as a rather one-dimensional character, a femme fatale who enriched herself by betraying the man who loved her.

Delilah may not have been an Israelite but a Philistine, which could have given her an added motive, beyond money, for betraying her lover. The Philistines were seafaring people who had emigrated from the Aegean and had settled along the coast. Their knowledge of smelting and forging metal, including iron, allowed them to rule over southwestern Canaan. As such, they became Israel's long-term enemies. Some years later, David killed the giant Philistine warrior Goliath. Later, the Philistine army defeated King Saul and his son Jonathan. The word *Palestine* is derived from their name, though the first historical record of the term doesn't appear until the fifth century BC, and it wasn't used to refer to the region until the second century AD.

At the end of his life, blinded and enslaved by his enemies, Samson asked for God's help and received it. How ironic that the Philistines met their deaths at the very moment they were thanking their god for having delivered their enemy Samson into their hands.

The pattern of Samson's life and his fatal attraction to the soulless beauty, Delilah, mirrors Israel's own unfaithfulness to the God who called his people and set them apart as his own. The story of Delilah and her brute of a boyfriend, Samson, reminds us of God's ability to engineer the least likely circumstances and the most flawed people to accomplish his plan to deliver us.

DELILAH'S *Legacy* IN SCRIPTURE

READ
Judges 16:4-5

Beyond the obvious reason, why would Delilah betray Samson? What did she hope to gain?

READ
Judges 16:6-16

How did Delilah wear Samson down until he told her the truth of his strength? Delilah was nothing if not persistent. How is persistence a negative here? When is persistence a good thing?

READ
Judges 16:17-22

- What character traits would you assign to Delilah? Does she have any redeeming qualities?

- Why would God choose to work through a woman like Delilah and a man like Samson? What does this say about God?

- At the end of Delilah's story, it seems that evil has won. However, Samson finally triumphs. How might this narrative give you faith in a God who keeps his promises?

OUR *Connection* TO DELILAH

The Philistines offered Delilah the unimaginable sum of fifty-five hundred shekels to betray her lover. (Joseph was sold for twenty and Jesus for thirty shekels.) Unlike Jael, who was considered a hero for eliminating an enemy of Israel, the villainess Delilah destroyed the man God had chosen to deliver his people. And deliver them he did!

- If you were to think of Delilah as a multifaceted character, what fears or insecurities do you imagine might have motivated her?

- Delilah served as a snare to a man who was chosen by God to lead his people. What kind of snares do you face in your efforts to live for God?

- The story of Delilah and her strong/weak lover, Samson, exposed a time of great weakness among God's people. How might it provide some consolation in times when the church itself seems weak?

God, how easy it is to consider wicked Delilah and weak Samson and quickly assume I'd never be like them. Rescue me, Lord, from my own tendency to stray from you. Remind me that only in relationship with you can I find the strength to stay the course until the end.

WEEK 16

NAOMI

"MY JOY" OR "PLEASANT"

Her Story

Naomi went to Moab with a husband and two sons, and there all three died. She returned to Bethlehem a bitter woman, accompanied only by her daughter-in-law Ruth.

"Don't call me Naomi," she told them. "Call me Mara, because the Almighty has made my life very bitter." RUTH 1:20

READ

Ruth 1-4

Who WAS SHE?

After moving to Moab to escape a famine, Naomi reintroduced herself to the women of Bethlehem with a new name that meant "bitter." While away, she had lost her husband and both sons. When her daughter-in-law Ruth cared for her devotedly and bravely, for she was a foreign woman entering fields filled with Israelite men, and then gave her a grandson, her joy returned. The women of Bethlehem went so far as to say that Ruth "loves you and . . . is better to you than seven sons" (Ruth 4:15).

A *Closer Look* AT NAOMI'S STORY

HER STORY TOOK PLACE AROUND 1200–1100 BC.

By now you might realize that many of the early biblical narratives are stories about founding families and the extended families, clans, tribes, and nations that sprang from them. Beginning with Adam and Eve, the Bible makes no effort to hide how dysfunctional many of these families were. For example, an incestuous relationship between Abraham's nephew Lot and Lot's elder daughter resulted in the nation of Moab, mentioned in Naomi's story.

The destruction of Sodom and Gomorrah—and Lot's wife along with them—reduced Lot's once prosperous family to living in a cave. Despairing of ever being able to marry and have children, Lot's daughters got their father drunk and slept with him. While the elder gave birth to Moab, the younger gave birth to Ben-Ammi, from whom the Ammonites descended (Genesis 19:36-38). These Moabites and Ammonites would later oppose the Israelite invasion of Canaan and remained Israel's enemies throughout most of its early history.

Hundreds of years later, in a time of relative peace, Naomi and her husband and sons fled a famine in Bethlehem and moved to Moab, which was located to the east of the Dead Sea in what is today west-central Jordan. In the rich highlands of Moab, rivers and rainfall provided enough food for everyone. But while living there, heartache struck Naomi not once but three times. Her husband died first, and then her two grown sons. But she still had two Moabite daughters-in-law, both of whom loved her and wanted to return with her to Bethlehem.

Naomi knew the only thing worse than a widow without children was three childless widows. With no male relatives to support her, a widow could become destitute, forced to sell herself into slavery or prostitution to survive. Even though God had commanded his people to care for widows, they often ignored the Mosaic laws, especially during the time of the judges, when Naomi's story took place.

She may also have felt it dangerous to bring Moabite women with her, lest they came to harm. Some Israelites might have viewed them as temptresses who would influence men to commit idolatry (Numbers 25:1-2).

Fortunately, Ruth insisted on following Naomi to Bethlehem. At the end of the story, we see Naomi not as an embittered, lonely, impoverished old woman but as a woman surrounded by family, in a scene of domestic bliss. Through Ruth she gained a son-in-law, a grandchild, and the praise of the women of Bethlehem, who blessed her, saying: "May [your grandson] become famous throughout Israel! He will renew your life and sustain you in your old age" (Ruth 4:14–15).

NAOMI'S *Legacy* IN SCRIPTURE

READ

Ruth 1

- Compare Naomi's two names: Naomi (meaning "pleasant") and Mara (meaning "bitter"). What do these names reveal about Naomi's mental state? How did Naomi feel about God's part in her triple tragedy? Read the text carefully for evidence.

- How is Naomi's assessment of God's role accurate or inaccurate?

- In her bitter circumstances, how did Naomi treat her widowed daughters-in-law?

- What reaction might Naomi have had when Ruth insisted on staying with her? Consider the range of emotions she might have experienced.

- The Hebrew word *hesed* is used three times in Ruth, twice by Naomi (Ruth 1:8; 2:20) and once by Boaz (Ruth 3:10). All three times it is translated "kindness." Discuss Naomi's use of the word and what it reveals about her understanding of God despite her tragic circumstances.

- When you think of Naomi, do you think of her as strong or weak? Defend your answer.

- Would you be strong or weak in Naomi's circumstances? How might such heartbreak affect your relationship with and understanding of God?

OUR *Connection* TO NAOMI

Naomi's misfortunes convinced her God was against her. Boaz's kindness revived her heart, enabling her to believe that God had not stopped showing his loving-kindness to her.

- Though God sometimes renamed people in the Bible, Naomi renamed herself: "Don't call me Naomi [meaning "pleasant"] . . . Call me Mara [meaning "bitter"], because the Almighty has made my life very bitter" (Ruth 1:20). What does this reveal about her view of God? How would you rename yourself based on your own circumstances?

- Naomi wrestled honestly with her feelings. Have you ever felt that your past hardships were evidence of God's displeasure? Do you see it any differently now?

- God's surprising provision took time. Naomi's blessings overflowed from her to God's people through her grandson Obed. How has God surprised you with his provision and care in your own life?

Almighty God, the same One who helped Naomi, give me the grace and strength to trust you even in life's most trying circumstances. Help me always to remember that you love me and will work all things for my good, just as you did for Naomi.

WEEK 17

RUTH

"FRIEND," "COMPANION," OR "VISION OF BEAUTY"

Her Story

A young widow without children, Ruth followed her mother-in-law to Bethlehem rather than stay in her native Moab.

When Naomi realized that Ruth was determined to go with her, she stopped urging her. RUTH 1:18

READ

Ruth 1-4

Who WAS SHE?

An exceptionally kind and loyal young woman from Moab, Ruth married Naomi's younger son, Kilion. Naomi's husband had already died, and now both of her sons had died as well, leaving three widowed women—Naomi, Orpah, and Ruth. When Naomi decided to return to her roots in Bethlehem, Orpah stayed in Moab. However, Ruth couldn't bear to leave the mother-in-law she had come to love. Her famous words of commitment to Naomi and Naomi's God have echoed in hearts for thousands of years.

A Closer Look AT RUTH'S STORY

HER STORY TOOK PLACE AROUND 1200–1050 BC.

Amazing Ruth! She is one of the few individuals in the Bible who seemed to respond perfectly to the challenges placed before her.

Like Naomi, she was a grieving widow without children. But instead of becoming infected with Naomi's depression, believing that God had turned against her, Ruth upended everything by proclaiming her allegiance to Naomi and her God.

Most people in the Ancient Near East worshiped gods with limited jurisdictions. These gods were active in certain geographic regions and localities, but not everywhere. Some were thought to have influence over the sea, others over the sky, and still others over the harvest. But Israel's God was different. He possessed unlimited and universal authority.

Ruth would have learned about Naomi's God after marrying into the family. By leaving Moab behind, she said goodbye not only to her own people but also to their religious beliefs.

In their shared difficulties, the two women became like mother and daughter. Later, when Ruth took Naomi's advice and went to lie down at Boaz's feet while he was sleeping outside on the threshing floor, she took a huge risk. After the work was done, the threshers would feast and drink heartily and then bed down for the night to guard the harvest. Though a male stronghold, the threshing floor at night sometimes attracted prostitutes. When Boaz awoke and Ruth asked him to "spread the corner of your garment over me, since you are a guardian-redeemer of our family" (Ruth 3:9), she was asking him to marry her.

Previously, when Ruth gleaned in his fields, Boaz had spoken a blessing over her, saying, "May you be richly rewarded by the LORD, the God of Israel, under whose wings you have come to take refuge" (Ruth 2:12). When Ruth used the phrase "corner of your garment," she used a Hebrew word (*kanap*), which can also be translated as "wings," meaning she asked Boaz for refuge in marriage.

As a widow, Ruth had the right to appeal to a guardian-redeemer, or *go'el*, to act on her behalf. In such cases, the closest male relative was expected to rescue or deliver her by paying off debts or buying back properties that had been sold, because without land people could barely survive.

As it happens, Ruth's guardian-redeemer, Boaz, was a descendant of Rahab, the woman who protected the Jewish spies in Jericho. Like Rahab, Ruth was an outsider who became an insider because of how God worked in her life. Instead of a foreigner and temptress, she is remembered as a hero in Israel. In addition to being the beloved daughter-in-law of Naomi, wife of Boaz, and mother of Obed, she is the great-grandmother of King David. Ruth is also mentioned in the genealogy of Jesus (Matthew 1:5), and her story foreshadows his role as both our Guardian-Redeemer and beloved Bridegroom.

Ruth's *Legacy* in Scripture

READ

Ruth 1:11-18

- Give as many reasons as you can for why Ruth may have wanted to stay with Naomi.

- First Naomi was a refugee in Moab. Then Ruth was a refugee in Israel. What might be similar and what might be different about refugees then and now?

READ

Ruth 2

- How did God's commands (Leviticus 19:9-10; 23:22; Deuteronomy 24:19) protect women like Naomi and Ruth?

- What sort of danger might Ruth have been in and why (note especially Ruth 2:9, 22)?

READ
Ruth 3

- What was Ruth's bold and brave action that night on the threshing floor? What does she want from Boaz?

- What does Boaz's response to Ruth tell you about him?

- Like Ruth, how might you show kindness to an older woman who is alone and needy?

OUR *Connection* TO RUTH

Ruth's declaration to Naomi, "Where you go I will go, and where you stay I will stay" (Ruth 1:16), is often invoked at weddings. How beautiful is this declaration of loyalty between two women from two different cultures!

- Ruth just happened to choose Boaz's field. When have you experienced something that seemed more than a coincidence?

- Boaz hoped God would repay Ruth's kindness (Ruth 2:12), never suspecting that he would become the answer to his own prayer. How have you become the answer to your own prayer or someone else's?

- Ruth's story is marked by a series of blessings. First she blessed Naomi by refusing to leave her. Then Naomi blessed Ruth by helping her find a husband. Then Boaz blessed Ruth with a home, and God blessed them both with a child. In what ways has God blessed you and made you a blessing to others?

Father, where you go, I will go.
Wherever you are, that's where I want to be.
Your people will be my people,
And you will always be my God.
Help me to follow you steadfastly all my life,
And when I die, receive me to yourself.

WEEK 18

HANNAH

"GRACIOUSNESS" OR "FAVOR"

Her Story

Hannah begged God for a child with such anguish and tears that a nearby priest thought she was drunk.

Eli answered, "Go in peace, and may the God of Israel grant you what you have asked of him." 1 SAMUEL 1:17

READ

1 Samuel 1:1-2:11, 18-21

Who WAS SHE?

Although she was her husband's favorite wife, Hannah felt the sting of being childless, a pain made sharper by her rival Peninnah's cruel jabs. After Hannah's impassioned prayer, God finally gave her a son whom she named Samuel, which in Hebrew sounds like "heard by God." After his birth, Hannah left him at the tabernacle in the care of the old priest, Eli. Since Samuel had just been weaned, he may have been about three years old. By consecrating him to God, Hannah understood the sacred nature of the promise she had made when imploring God for a child.

A *Closer Look* AT HANNAH'S STORY

HER STORY TOOK PLACE AROUND 1120–1100 BC.

After Joshua led the Israelites on their initial conquest of the promised land, he erected a tabernacle at Shiloh, about twenty miles north of Jerusalem. For more than three hundred years, it served as the religious center of the new nation. It was eventually supplanted by the magnificent temple King Solomon built in Jerusalem.

Like the surrounding peoples, the Israelites had developed a sacrificial system of worship, which was dictated by the laws God had given to Moses. More than giving something away, as we tend to think of sacrifices, they would have thought of giving something *over*. Sacrifice always involved transformation. Whatever was given in sacrifice was transformed because it was transferred from the common realm to the realm of the sacred.

When Hannah and her husband brought their sacrifices to God at Shiloh, they were returning to him gifts he had given them—animals, grain, and wine. Later, Hannah would give over Samuel, the son with whom God had blessed her, so he could serve at Shiloh.

When Hannah poured out her heart to God, the old priest Eli, one of the last of the judges, concluded she was drunk. Spiritually dense and morally compromised by his failure to discipline his sons (1 Samuel 2:12-17, 22-25), Eli had a difficult time distinguishing flesh from Spirit, much like the people who would later accuse Jesus' disciples of drunkenness after the Spirit filled them at Pentecost (Acts 2:4, 13).

Hannah was one of Elkanah's two wives. In the early history of Israel, the practice of polygamy was generally reserved for wealthy families. Rather than stemming from uncontrolled sexual desire, husbands more commonly practiced polygamy to continue the family line and to produce a family large enough to handle the labor-intensive demands of farming and raising livestock.

Unlike Eli, Samuel grew up to become a great man of God. The last of the judges and a prophet, he anointed Saul as Israel's first king as well as David, Israel's greatest king.

Hannah's beautiful prayer, commemorated in 1 Samuel 2:1-10, was echoed centuries later by another young mother (Luke 1:46-55). Like Hannah's child, the infant growing inside Mary would be born in answer to prayer, and he would be destined to cause the falling and rising of many in Israel (Luke 2:34).

HANNAH'S *Legacy* IN SCRIPTURE

READ
1 Samuel 1:1-20

- Why was Hannah not able to have a child?

- What made the pain of her infertility even worse?

- What vow did Hannah make if God would give her a son? What would fulfilling that vow look like? What would it feel like?

- What response do you have to Elkanah's offer of comfort when Hannah weeps (1 Samuel 1:8)?

- Why was Hannah no longer "downcast" (1 Samuel 1:18) after her encounter with the priest Eli?

READ
1 Samuel 1:21-28

- Discuss your own emotions when you read what Hannah did in fulfillment of her vow. What does this tell you about her?

READ

1 Samuel 2:18-26

- How did God bless Hannah for keeping her vow?

- Compare 1 Samuel 2:26 and Luke 2:52. What is the same between these verses? What is different, and why?

OUR *Connection* TO HANNAH

Instead of becoming resentful and embittered, Hannah poured out her deeply troubled soul to the only one who could help her. Her powerful prayer rose up to God and resulted in a complete reversal of fortune. Her son Samuel led God's people from the chaotic period of the judges to the establishment of the monarchy.

- Note how Hannah dealt with Peninnah's taunts in 1 Samuel 1:6–7. How do you respond to difficult people?

- How might the understanding of sacrifice as transformation, as "giving over" rather than "giving away," affect your willingness to sacrifice something to God?

- Hannah's song in 1 Samuel 2:1–10 emphasizes a series of reversals. What are these reversals, and what does she mean by saying, "It is not by strength that one prevails" (1 Samuel 2:9)? How might your life or perspective change if you took this statement seriously?

Lord, teach me how to pray when I'm disappointed and hurting. Even more, please teach me how to live for you even when your plans do not align with my wishes. Help me to discover the contentment that comes from wanting your will more than my own.

WEEK 19

MICHAL

"WHO IS LIKE GOD?"

Her Story

Michal felt ashamed of David as he danced with abandon before God, and she belittled him.

Michal daughter of Saul watched from a window. And when she saw King David leaping and dancing before the Lord, she despised him in her heart. 2 SAMUEL 6:16

READ

1 Samuel 18:20-29; 19:11-17; 25:44; 2 Samuel 6:16-23

Who WAS SHE?

A young princess in Israel's new royal family, Michal must have been accustomed to getting what she wanted. And what she wanted was an attractive young warrior by the name of David. She was "in love," the Bible tells us (1 Samuel 18:20). Many places in the Bible honor marital love, but this is the only verse that explicitly mentions a woman being "in love" with a man. Michal's father, King Saul, gave her what she wanted, but only because he hoped to trap David into a contest that would get him killed. A pawn in the hands of the men in her life, Michal struggled to be more than a victim of her circumstances.

A *Closer Look* AT MICHAL'S STORY

HER STORY TOOK PLACE AROUND 1050–1000 BC.

Michal lived during a time of great transition, a period in which Israel moved from the era of the judges to that of the monarchy. Israel's first kings, Saul and David, had defeated many of their surrounding enemies, something that hadn't happened under the disorganized reign of the judges.

By then, many of the region's great powers—the Hittites, Assyrians, Babylonians, and Egyptians—were consumed with internal problems that prevented them from asserting more influence. That gave Saul and David the opportunity to extend Israel's borders. Only the Philistines, who lived along the coast, proved too hard to dislodge.

Hannah's son Samuel, Israel's last judge, anointed Saul as Israel's first king. But it wasn't long before Saul proved himself unworthy by repeatedly disobeying God. Even though Saul reproduced the pattern in Judges by doing "what was right in his own eyes" (Judges 21:25 ESV), he reigned for forty-two years, until he committed suicide to avoid capture by the Philistines.

David ruled for an additional forty years, and his son Solomon ruled for forty more. After that, the nation was divided into the Southern Kingdom of Judah and the Northern Kingdom of Israel.

Though Michal's story began like a fairy tale—she was a princess who married a hero—it ended tragically. Her father tried to use her as a snare to David and then gave her to another man after David fled. After Saul's death, she was bartered back to David by her brother.

Before she was very old, Michal had already lost two husbands as well as her father and three brothers who had fallen while fighting the Philistines. Then her brother Ishbosheth was murdered by his own men. As David consolidated his power, Michal's alienation seems to have grown to the point that she began acting more like Saul's daughter than David's wife. When he danced in public to celebrate the ark of the covenant's return to its proper place in Jerusalem, she met him with scorn.

Her sad tale ends on a gloomy note. Living in David's palace, she remained who she had always been, a princess and then a queen—a pretty bird confined to a royal cage, merely a tool of powerful men. Childless until her death, Michal had no one to "arise and call her blessed" (Proverbs 31:28).

The Bible doesn't indicate whether Michal was childless because of barrenness or because David refused to sleep with her. As Israel's new king, he may have wanted to control her fertility, thus ensuring there would be no rival claimants to his throne from the house of Saul. Those who heard Michal's story would probably have considered her childlessness a curse.

MICHAL'S *Legacy* IN SCRIPTURE

READ

1 Samuel 18:20-29; 19:11-17; 25:44;
2 Samuel 3:14-16; 6:14-23

- Go through these passages verse by verse and list Michal's qualities based on the events.

- How did Michal's father treat her and her husband David and how did that affect her?

- What happened to Michal after she helped David escape? Nine years later, David demanded her back. How do you think this shaped her opinion of David?

- Why didn't Michal understand David's need to dance and praise God with abandon?

- Are you a spectator or a participant in worship? What needs to happen to bring you to a place where you can worship God with the focus on him rather than on yourself?

OUR *Connection* TO MICHAL

Michal is a complicated character who suffered greatly because she was caught in the tension between two kings. She loved David enough to lie to her enraged father out of loyalty to him, but she later treated David with contempt. What anguish she must have felt, as an unloved princess trapped in a palace with no children, family, or friends to comfort her.

- Born to royal privilege, Michal was a pawn of powers she could not control. What parts of her story impact you most? In what ways, if any, can you relate to her?

- Over the course of her life, Michal experienced tremendous loss. Her grief and bitterness must have made it difficult for her to move into a renewed relationship with David, even though he had been her first love. How have your own hardships affected your relationships, even your relationship with God?

God, my heart is broken for Michal and for every woman victimized by those who are more powerful than they are. Give me a heart to help and to pray for these women, so that they may have victory in you.

WEEK 20

ABIGAIL

"MY FATHER IS JOY"

Her Story

Wife of a foolish man, she faced down an angry David and his mob of men intent on killing her family.

When Abigail saw David, she . . . . fell at his feet and said: "Pardon your servant, my lord, and let me speak to you; hear what your servant has to say." 1 SAMUEL 25:23–24

READ

1 Samuel 25:2–42

Who WAS SHE?

Most readers will find it easy to admire Abigail's bravery and resourcefulness. She ignored the commands of her foolish husband, gathered all the food and more that he had refused to give David and his men, tracked them down, then bowed to the ground before the young warrior in a position of total humility and defenselessness. Her words and actions diffused David's anger and saved her family. Then, in a part of her story that reads a bit like a romance novel, she became the wife of the future king of Israel and bore him a son (2 Samuel 3:3).

A *Closer Look* AT ABIGAIL'S STORY

HER STORY TOOK PLACE AROUND 1025–1000 BC.

As the wife of a wealthy landowner whose herds would have produced significant income, Abigail presided over a large household. Her ability to get her hands on so much food at such short notice, and the fact that she had servants to command as well as five maids who traveled with her when she married David, are evidence of her wealth.

While Abigail took care of the household, her husband Nabal would have been responsible for hiring shepherds to care for his large flocks. Each shepherd would receive meat, milk, and a negotiated portion of the wool at shearing time. Often shepherds had to lead their flocks a considerable distance in search of pasture, which would have made their sheep more vulnerable to attack by wild animals or marauders.

Normal birth and attrition rates were calculated, and sheep that had been lost due to predators or illness had to be accounted for by bringing the owner some part of the animal, like skin, tendons, or ears. The shepherd would be expected to make up any losses according to previously agreed upon terms.

Though Nabal was a wealthy man who could well afford the protection David and his men provided, his greatest asset was his beautiful and intelligent wife, Abigail. But what a liability that foolish man was to her! Though God dealt decisively with Nabal, Abigail's subsequent marriage to David held its own share of dangers.

When Abigail first met him, David was an outlaw hiding in the wilderness from King Saul, along with his fighting men and their families. Imagine how much she gave up by joining him there. One day, when David and his men were away, she and the other women and children were abducted by Amalekite raiders. How terrified they must have been as they waited for David to rescue them (1 Samuel 30:1-20).

Abigail and David had a son named Kileab (also called Daniel). She was probably living in Jerusalem with David when Michal was forcibly returned to him.

In contrast to Michal, who had little control over her life, in a time of crisis Abigail was able to both speak and act independently and with wisdom. By acting at the right moment in just the right way, she prevented her household from being slaughtered and kept the future King David from shedding innocent blood.

ABIGAIL'S *Legacy* IN SCRIPTURE

READ

1 Samuel 25:2-42

- Compare Abigail's character with Nabal's. Why would she choose to marry such a man?

- What caused David to respond with such anger and potential violence?

- What are your thoughts about the servant who went behind Nabal's back and told Abigail what had happened? Take special note of the last sentence in his report.

- Abigail bows with her face to the ground in a position of surrender and humility—and danger—when she encounters David and his men. Was this wise or foolish or both?

- What argument from Abigail convinces David to abandon his need for revenge? Why is this important?

- When and how have you been like each character in this story? Foolish Nabal? Wise and quick-acting Abigail? Vengeful David?

OUR *Connection* TO ABIGAIL

Leah and Rachel, Jacob's wives, must have been terrified as Esau and his four hundred men advanced (Genesis 33:1–3). But Abigail had to face the outlaw David and his four hundred men by herself. Courageous and quick-witted, she acted like Jacob, who pacified Esau by sending gifts in advance of their meeting (Genesis 32:9–18). Abigail's honesty and humility pacified David and restrained his anger, preventing him from becoming like Esau, the man who had lost his birthright.

- Genesis 2:18 indicates that Eve was created to be an *ezer*, a delivering ally, for Adam. How did Abigail play this role for David, and how might he have been affected had she not?

- Though provoked, neither Abigail nor David took revenge on Nabal. What does the story reveal about their character and their relationship to God?

- **Abigail was a peacemaker. How have you been called to bring peace to difficult situations, and what did you learn from trying to do that?**

Lord, make me an instrument of your peace. Remind me not to sow seeds of discord. Instead, help me to sow seeds of love and hope and joy in your name.

WEEK 21

THE WOMAN OF ENDOR

Her Story

A medium, she saw through Saul's disguise and treated him kindly when discerning his imminent death.

"Now please listen to your servant and let me give you some food so you may eat and have the strength to go on your way." 1 SAMUEL 28:22

READ
1 Samuel 28

Who WAS SHE?

Though practicing any kind of witchcraft carried a death sentence in Israel, this woman in Endor did as a desperate King Saul had asked. She brought up the dead prophet Samuel, the very one whose words Saul had ignored while he was alive. Samuel's words so disturbed the woman that she reacted with compassion for Saul, urging him to sit down for a meal that would strengthen him for the deadly events that lay ahead.

A *Closer Look* AT THE WOMAN OF ENDOR'S STORY

HER STORY TOOK PLACE AROUND 1010 BC.

This mysterious woman, who laid claim to otherworldly powers, encountered Saul on the night before his death, long after the apex of his power. As Israel's first monarch, King Saul was supposed to become the ideal ruler, breaking the mold of selfish and arrogant earthly kings. Rather than becoming a law to himself, he was to rule humbly under God's direction. But Saul had his own ideas. Whenever the prophet Samuel conveyed God's instructions, Saul found excuses to ignore them. Instead of trusting God, Saul trusted his gut, forging the sure and steady path that had led to this night.

During his reign, Saul had consulted the prophet Samuel for direction. But now Samuel was dead. He would also have consulted the Urim (likely means "lights") and Thummim (likely means "completeness") for revelation. These sacred objects may have been small sticks inscribed with symbols, or they may have been metal objects or stones carried in the breastplate and ephod worn by the high priest. They could be cast as lots so that God's will could be determined through a series of yes or no questions. But Saul had lost access to these when one of the priests took them to David while fleeing Saul's wrath (1 Samuel 22:19-23; 23:9).

The primary role of spiritists or mediums was to communicate with the spirit world, especially to call up the dead. The Hebrew word for *medium* in this story is literally "ghostwife" or "ghostmistress." The Israelites believed that those who dabbled in the occult were engaging demonic powers and false gods to obtain hidden knowledge.

Though forbidden to the Israelites, necromancy—the practice of trying to communicate with the dead—was practiced throughout the Ancient Near East. Such attempts were usually motivated by fear or the desire for power. In this case, Saul was desperately afraid of the fate that awaited him on the battlefield. How ironic that his fears had reduced him to breaking his own law against consulting mediums!

The woman of Endor seemed startled when the prophet Samuel appeared to her. Perhaps she had always relied on pretense to convince her clients that she could communicate with the dead. Even though God allowed Samuel to appear in this eerie scene, the story was not meant to approve the practice of necromancy but only to highlight Saul's persistent foolishness and subsequent fate because he would not listen to God. Though sometimes called the "Witch of Endor" because of her claim to magical powers, this woman seemed genuinely moved by Saul's distress and the tragedy that would soon overtake him and his three sons in their battle with the Philistines.

THE WOMAN OF ENDOR'S *Legacy* IN SCRIPTURE

READ

1 Samuel 28:3-25

- When the woman saw Samuel, she realized her guest was King Saul. What so frightened her that she yelled "at the top of her voice" (1 Samuel 28:12)?

- Why would Saul ask for Samuel when he had disobeyed any command Samuel had ever given him?

- Do you think the person who appeared was actually the prophet Samuel or some spirit imitating him? Explain your answer.

- Have you ever dabbled in any sort of occult practice—even "just for fun"? What can you learn about such practices from this story?

- We tend to think of witches and occult practitioners as evil and mean. This woman's kindness to Saul adds another layer to the story. What might you learn from this?

OUR *Connection* TO THE WOMAN OF ENDOR

In her vision, the medium saw Samuel as "an old man wearing a robe" (an important detail in the story) (1 Samuel 28:14). When she saw the king's fear, she took pity on him. Acting like a generous hostess, she served him and his two companions a fatted calf and unleavened bread for their last meal.

- What phrase or sentence would you use to describe the woman of Endor?

- Robes were symbols of authority. Samuel's robe signified his authority as God's prophet. Saul, on the other hand, would have taken off his kingly robes to disguise himself. What is the significance of the enrobed prophet appearing to the robeless king (1 Samuel 15:22-29)?

- What does this strange episode reveal about the consequences of trusting yourself instead of God?

Ancient people believed the supernatural world was real. How is that worldview both affirmed and denied in our culture today? How does your understanding of the existence of the supernatural world shape your daily life?

Lord God, ruler of life and death, give me insight into your will and ways and the desire to obey you always. Forgive me when I reach out to false powers to gain a sense of security. My only security is in you, the Lord of my life.

WEEK 22

BATHSHEBA

"DAUGHTER OF THE OATH" OR "DAUGHTER OF SEVEN"
(SEVEN SYMBOLIZES PERFECTION)

Her Story

When brought to King David, Bathsheba became pregnant, and a royal crisis ensued.

Then David sent messengers to get [Bathsheba]. She came to him, and he slept with her. 2 SAMUEL 11:4

READ

2 Samuel 11:1-12:25

Who WAS SHE?

Bathsheba, wife of Uriah, has been portrayed both as a temptress and as a victim. Which was she? King David spotted her from the rooftop of his palace when she was taking her ritual bath. Their unlawful union led to the murder of one of David's best soldiers and a royal cover-up. As a result, a string of death and family dysfunction haunted David's house for many years.

A *Closer Look* AT BATHSHEBA'S STORY

HER STORY TOOK PLACE AROUND 990–950 BC.

When David was an outlaw in the Judean wilderness, Abigail intervened to prevent him from retaliating against her husband, Nabal. With her help, David passed an important test. Instead of using his growing power to wreak vengeance, he would use that power as God instructed.

Bathsheba's story emerged at a very different moment in David's life. No longer hiding from Saul in the wilderness, he was now Israel's undisputed king. Comfortable, powerful, secure, and restless—that was his condition when he faced another crucial test, this time at his palace in Jerusalem.

Notably, the story opens in the spring, "at the time when kings go off to war" (2 Samuel 11:1). In springtime, muddy roads became passable again and there was enough food to feed an army. The king's army had indeed gone off to war, but this time without the king. David's soldiers were encamped forty miles northeast at Rabbah, the Ammonite capital. While his men were laying siege to a city, David was at home napping.

Afterward, while walking on the palace roof, he spotted below him a beautiful woman taking a bath. Like a true son of Eve, who saw that fruit from the Tree of the Knowledge of Good and Evil was pleasing to the eye and desirable, David reached out his hand and took what he desired. After all, he was the king, wasn't he? It was as simple and as wicked as that.

David transgressed a law that even some pagan kings feared to break, knowing that the penalty for adultery was death. He also knew Bathsheba to be the wife of Uriah and the daughter of Eliam, two members of his elite royal guard—men he knew well. Her grandfather may even have been Ahithophel, David's close and wise counselor.

David's decision led to a cascade of tragedies—the murder of Bathsheba's husband Uriah and the soldiers with him, the death of Bathsheba and David's child, and later the deaths of three of David's sons.

Did Bathsheba love David? Had she agreed to the affair? Or had she felt compelled to obey the summons of her powerful king? Scholars have argued it both ways. In his clever and pointed parable, the prophet Nathan pictures her favorably, as an innocent lamb.

Bathsheba's bath likely marked the end of her menstrual period. That's why news of her pregnancy would have landed like a bomb. Clearly, David was the father of her child.

As the king discovered, sin has a velocity all its own, with one sin rushing headlong into another. How tragic for Bathsheba, for her husband and child, for David and his family, and for the entire nation of Israel when their king, one of the Bible's mightiest heroes, failed a test that could have made him truly and forever "a man after [God's] own heart" (1 Samuel 13:14; Acts 13:22). Though we don't know what was in Bathsheba's heart, we can imagine how she must have exulted years later when her son Solomon finally succeeded to David's throne.

BATHSHEBA'S *Legacy* IN SCRIPTURE

READ
2 Samuel 11:2-5

- What part might Bathsheba have played in these events? Victim? Blameless? Temptress? Something in between? Explain your answer.

- What do you think Bathsheba was expecting from David when she told him she was pregnant?

READ
2 Samuel 11:6-27

- What might Bathsheba have been experiencing while David tried to get Uriah to go to his wife and then later masterminded his death? Pay attention to 2 Samuel 11:26.

- What does this story tell you about the results of temptation, dishonesty, the misuse of authority, and the pain that can result?

- How can you protect yourself against temptation?

OUR *Connection* TO BATHSHEBA

Bathsheba is listed in the Gospel of Matthew's genealogy of Jesus (through Joseph) as "Uriah's wife" (Matthew 1:6). Naming her murdered husband highlights David's sin, indicating that Jesus was connected to a long line of broken men and women who desperately needed the gracious provision of a Savior.

- Bathsheba's story could have been ripped from the daily headlines—a powerful man sexually abuses a beautiful woman. It's not hard to imagine the destruction and heartbreak that follows when a person whom God loves is treated as an object of lust. What does Bathsheba's story tell us about how God feels about such victimization?

- In the Ancient Near East, the punishment for adultery was usually death. Our own society often trivializes or glamorizes sexual immorality, but with what results? What are some ways of resisting and transcending the cultural tide?

Jesus our Savior, how grateful we are for the ready forgiveness available to us if we sincerely repent of our sins. Thank you for your sacrifice that makes it possible. We praise you for your goodness and grace toward us.

WEEK 23

TAMAR

"DATE TREE" OR "PALM TREE"

Her Story

Tamar, the daughter of King David, was raped by her half brother Amnon, who then threw her out of his house and bolted the door.

Then Amnon hated her with intense hatred. In fact, he hated her more than he had loved her. Amnon said to her, "Get up and get out!" 2 SAMUEL 13:15

READ

2 Samuel 13:1-37

Who WAS SHE?

King David's daughter Tamar went to cheer up her half brother Amnon, only to have him rape her, an act that stole her innocence, virginity, and future. When he was finished with her, he had her thrown out of his house. Desolate and weeping, Tamar took refuge with her brother, Absalom. But Absalom compounded her misery by callously telling her not to take the incident to heart, as though that were possible. From that day on Tamar lived in her brother's house, her chances for marriage and family destroyed. Scripture's last words about Tamar call her "a desolate woman" (2 Samuel 13:20).

A *Closer Look* AT TAMAR'S STORY

HER STORY TOOK PLACE IN THE EARLY TENTH CENTURY BC.

David had nineteen sons by his many wives and yet more sons by his ten concubines. Tamar is the only one of his daughters named in the Bible. How tragic that she was raped by her half brother Amnon, the heir to David's throne.

To add to that atrocity, Tamar was doubly wounded because Amnon's crime likely made her unmarriageable, since she would have been considered damaged goods. Ironically, sexual violations were treated not only as crimes against women but against the property rights of fathers and husbands.

Though her brother, Absalom, eventually avenged her rape by killing his half brother Amnon, we hear nothing more of Tamar other than that she lived "in her brother Absalom's house, a desolate woman" (2 Samuel 13:20). The Hebrew word for "desolate" used here is *shomemah*, normally associated with ruined cities or lands laid waste by war. It's a chilling image of Tamar's emotional state. She had been hollowed out and socially erased, her future destroyed because of her brother's depravity and her father's unwillingness to confront and discipline his son.

God's word to David through the prophet Nathan had come true: "The sword will never depart from your house, because you despised me and took the wife of Uriah the Hittite to be your own" (2 Samuel 12:10). David's lack of moral authority enabled sin to continue winding its cancerous way through the royal family.

What a far cry Tamar's story is from the Eden ideal of men and women—created in God's image—ruling the earth together. Instead of being treated with equal dignity by her father, her brother, and the society in which she lived, Tamar was desecrated and abandoned. Her story is a reminder of how twisted the relationship between the sexes can become.

The practice of polygamy, which surfaced in Scripture just six generations after Adam (Genesis 4:17–19), distorted the ideal of one man and one woman united in marriage (Genesis 2:24; Matthew 19:4–5). Though the Old Testament never condemns polygamy, it usually portrays it negatively. In this case, David seemed unable or unwilling to discipline his many sons begotten with his many wives, with the result that one son committed rape and another committed murder, echoing the twin evils David had committed, first against Bathsheba and then against Uriah. A third son, Adonijah, was later executed by David's son Solomon for trying to steal the throne (1 Kings 1:5-53, 2:13-25).

Though women in Israel had far fewer rights than men, it's worth noting that whenever Old Testament commands diverged from the laws of other cultures, they tended to move in the direction of more equality between the sexes and greater respect for human life. Using the raw material he had at hand—broken men and women—God was gradually shaping his people toward justice.

Though Tamar was a royal princess, her brother ruined her life because he failed to respect her dignity as a woman made in God's image.

TAMAR'S *Legacy* IN SCRIPTURE

READ

2 Samuel 13:1-22

- The Bible says that Amnon "fell in love with Tamar" (2 Samuel 13:1). Do you think that is an accurate statement? Why or why not?

- Read aloud Tamar's pleas in 2 Samuel 13:12-14. Women throughout history have echoed Tamar's cries. How do her pleas cause you pain? How might her story incline you to support women like Tamar?

- What was the initial response of Tamar's brother, Absalom? How do you think he helped or hurt Tamar?

- As the father of both Tamar and Amnon, how could or should David have responded? Consider 2 Samuel 13:21 and the law of Moses in Deuteronomy 22:28-29.

- Why would God allow such an ugly story to be included in the Bible? What link might there be between this story and 2 Samuel 12:11?

OUR *Connection* TO TAMAR

Were we to possess a before-and-after photograph of Tamar, we would likely be shocked by the transformation. Surely her face would reflect the pain of her fractured heart. The story of her trauma may expose wounds in our own lives or in those we know who have been crushed by sexual violence. What to do with our sorrow? How to handle our rage? We can begin by bringing our uncensored feelings before God, asking him to be present with us.

- In "Letter from Birmingham Jail," Dr. Martin Luther King Jr. wrote, "Injustice anywhere is a threat to justice everywhere." How does this statement strike you in relation to Tamar's story?

How do you think God feels about what happened to Tamar? Ask him to show you. (Consider 2 Samuel 12:10; Psalm 140:12; Jeremiah 9:24; 21:12; Luke 18:7-8; 2 Corinthians 1:3-4.)

God of justice and compassion, Tamar's story breaks our hearts and makes us angry. We know her story is repeated every day in our broken world. Give us your compassion for those we know who have been shattered by sexual violence. Grant us wisdom as we help guide them to healing. Bring their abusers to justice and repentance.

WEEK 24

THE WISE WOMAN OF ABEL

Her Story

This woman's wise but grisly actions prevented her city from being destroyed by David's armies.

"Hand over this one man, and I'll withdraw from the city." The woman said to Joab, "His head will be thrown to you from the wall." 2 SAMUEL 20:21

READ

2 Samuel 20:1-7, 14-22

Who WAS SHE?

In a place known for its ancient wisdom, one wise woman stepped forward to save a town that harbored a troublemaker rebelling against King David. From Benjamin, the tribe of former King Saul, Sheba had led a rebellion against David. All except the tribe of Judah had sided with Sheba. When chased by David's general Joab, Sheba took refuge in the town of Abel Beth Maakah. Joab besieged the town until a wise woman came forward and offered to turn over Sheba if Joab would leave. Recognizing an opportunity that would save his soldiers from death and a town from destruction, Joab accepted, and the gruesome deed was done.

A *Closer Look* AT THE WISE WOMAN OF ABEL'S STORY

HER STORY TOOK PLACE AROUND 1000 BC.

After Absalom avenged Tamar's rape, he led a failed rebellion against his father, David. In the aftermath of Absalom's death, a rebel from King Saul's tribe led an additional rebellion. When chased by Joab, this rebel holed up in Abel, a town located in Northern Israel, on the border between modern-day Syria, Lebanon, and Israel. The man's name was Sheba son of Bikri.

Determined to stamp out this latest rebellion and return Israel to stability, Joab, the commander of David's army, launched a siege against Abel. He began by building a ramp against the city walls. But his advance was interrupted by an unnamed woman boldly calling his name from her position atop the walls.

But why a woman? Why did Joab listen? And why, considering what an easy target he would have made, did he draw close to the city walls when she beckoned? It's likely that Joab, the same general who purposely placed Bathsheba's husband too close to another city's walls to ensure his death, recognized her as a "wise woman," someone acting in a semi-official capacity on behalf of the city. He knew he could safely approach because their impromptu parley would have afforded a time-out from the violence.

"Wise woman" may or may not have been an official title in the time of the judges and Israel's early monarchy. Regardless, in a society where women's authority was usually confined to the domestic sphere, this woman must have been someone of exceptional wisdom who possessed outstanding problem-solving skills.

Like Abigail facing down David and his four hundred men, the wise woman of Abel led with humility, announcing herself as Joab's servant. Then she confidently declared Abel's political position. Rather than rising in rebellion, the city remained faithful to David. Moreover, Abel was a place where people came to receive help for making important decisions and settling difficult disputes. Why would Joab want to destroy such a wise, peaceable, and faithful city, which was surely an asset in David's kingdom?

When Joab responded by saying he was only after one man—the troublemaker Sheba—she instantly announced the solution: "His head will be thrown to you from the wall" (2 Samuel 20:21). Rallying the town, she made good on her word, which prevented Joab from destroying his own people. With the trophy of Sheba's head in his hands, Joab halted the siege, dispersed his army, and returned to the king in Jerusalem. Because of one wise woman's confident assertion of authority and quick action to save her people, Joab no longer needed to breach Abel's walls, and many lives were spared.

THE WISE WOMAN OF ABEL'S *Legacy* IN SCRIPTURE

READ

2 Samuel 20:14-22

- Describe the scene when this woman appeared (2 Samuel 20:15-17). What character traits did she display even before wisdom?

- What about this woman's actions could be considered wise?

- Even considering the brutal facts of this story, how do you think she was a peacemaker?

- Review the woman's speech to Joab one phrase at a time. How do you see her wisely leading Jacob to the desired conclusion?

- What principles did she use, short of violence, that you might employ to diffuse a difficult or dangerous situation?

- Where can you go to develop wisdom in your own life?

OUR *Connection* TO THE WISE WOMAN OF ABEL

Her story resonates with thematic strands from the stories of Abigail, Esther, Rahab, and Deborah, with a little bit of Jael thrown in. Though the details differ, the same qualities prove vital. She was intelligent, persuasive, brave, diplomatic, quick-witted, and unafraid to do what had to be done to protect the lives of God's people.

- James 1:5 says, "If any of you lacks wisdom, you should ask God, who gives generously to all without finding fault, and it will be given to you." How might praying as James exhorts help you to become more like this woman?

- How does her story redefine the kind of leadership that is sometimes exercised outside the usual channels of power and authority?

Jesus, often I feel less than wise, unable to make hard decisions, unsure which way to go, incapable of moving forward with courage. You've promised to give us wisdom when we ask. I'm asking now. Give me a full measure of your wisdom.

WEEK 25

RIZPAH

"HOT STONE" OR "COAL"

Her Story

For six months Rizpah kept faithful watch over the dead and decomposing bodies of her sons and Saul's grandsons.

From the beginning of the harvest till the rain poured down from the heavens on the bodies, [Rizpah] did not let the birds touch them by day or the wild animals by night. 2 SAMUEL 21:10

READ

2 Samuel 21: 1–14

Who WAS SHE?

Was Rizpah sensible or foolish? Wise or crazy? To a casual observer, she might have looked crazy as she spread out sackcloth as a sign of mourning, then shouted, leaped, and waved her arms to fend off the birds and animals that would otherwise desecrate these royal bodies. Her sorrow pushed action to an extreme. Rizpah guarded the bodies as they wasted away in the heat of the day and the cool of the night, protecting them with her love, both fierce and wild.

A *Closer Look* AT RIZPAH'S STORY

HER STORY TOOK PLACE AROUND 1000–1050 BC.

Rizpah's long and agonized protest took place during an extended drought when David was king.

As King Saul's concubine, she was the mother of two of his sons. Now Saul was dead, killed the day after his strange encounter with the woman of Endor when he fell on his sword to evade capture by the Philistines. Robbed of a living trophy, the Philistines celebrated their victory by pinning his corpse, along with those of three of his sons, to a city wall. Grieved by Saul's death, allies from a nearby town snatched the royal bodies away in the middle of the night and then burned them to avoid further desecration. Then they buried their bones under a tamarisk tree.

When Saul died, Rizpah must have felt herself at a loss. The risk to her and her sons would have surged when David became king. Why would he allow potential rivals to remain alive? But thankfully, he did.

Until the famine that resulted from the drought.

When David inquired of the Lord about why there had been no rain, it was revealed that the drought had been caused by Saul's failure to abide by the treaty the Israelites had made with the Gibeonites when the Israelites had first entered the land (Joshua 9). Hoping to make things right, David asked the Gibeonites how he could atone for the violent way Saul had treated them.

Instead of money for payment, they took seven of Saul's male descendants and executed them, leaving their bodies exposed at Gibeah, Saul's hometown and the place where he had been anointed king. Rizpah's sons were swept up along with five of David's grandsons. Conveniently for David, their execution left alive only the lame Mephibosheth, an unlikely challenger to the throne. Since the number seven symbolized perfection, or completion, the Gibeonites would have considered Saul's offense atoned for perfectly.

But someone thought otherwise. Rizpah refused to hide either her grief or her opinion about what had taken place. Instead, she planted herself on a rock overspread with sackcloth, where she would live for the next six months. Rather than fleeing from so gruesome a sight, she stayed with the executed men, protecting their bodies from wild animals at night and birds of prey during the day.

When word of her fierce protest finally reached David, he arranged for the men to be buried. What's more, he gathered up the remains of Saul and his sons and had them buried in the tomb of Saul's father.

Only then did the rains return.

RIZPAH'S *Legacy* IN SCRIPTURE

READ

2 Samuel 21:1-14

- Why did Rizpah protect these bodies? What did she hope to accomplish?

- Rizpah stayed at her near-to-impossible task for about six months. Why didn't she give up? What do you think kept her going?

- Why did David wait so long to bury these sons of Saul? What finally made him take action?

- What might induce you to do something important, but scary or difficult, with the same passion and determination Rizpah displayed?

- Name four ways that God's love for you is like Rizpah's love for her sons.

OUR *Connection* TO RIZPAH

What might Rizpah have been thinking when she camped out from mid-April to early October, objecting to what had happened to her sons? Did she rage? Did she pray? Did God speak to her? How did she cope? Perhaps she realized that though God had revealed the reason for the drought, he had not prescribed the violent remedy. That was on David and the Gibeonites. What we do know is that her vigil paid off. Maybe then the Israelites realized that rain didn't fall after an act of violence but only after her act of devotion and David's act of reconciliation.

- How might Rizpah's example inspire you to persevere when you are called to confront something that is wrong?

- How do you relate to Rizpah's experience of grief or standing alone because of witnessing some kind of injustice, large or small?

God of justice, help me to confront injustice in my own time with the fervor and courage of Rizpah. I know not all battles are mine to fight, but show me the ones that are.

WEEK 26

THE QUEEN OF SHEBA

Her Story

The Queen of Sheba had heard rumors about Solomon's wisdom, wealth, and wonder-working God, so she traveled to Israel to see for herself.

When the queen of Sheba heard about the fame of Solomon and his relationship to the LORD, she came to test Solomon with hard questions. 1 KINGS 10:1

READ

1 Kings 10:1-13; Matthew 12:42

Who WAS SHE?

The Queen of Sheba entered Jerusalem trailed by a long line of camels carrying splendid gifts for King Solomon. With her she brought every question her sharp mind could devise. She discovered a king whose wisdom and wealth were unmatched, as Solomon satisfactorily answered each question and astonished her with the brilliant display of his riches.

A *Closer Look* AT THE QUEEN OF SHEBA'S STORY

HER STORY TOOK PLACE AROUND 970–931 BC.

To reach Jerusalem from her home in Sheba (modern-day Yemen), the Queen of Sheba likely traveled the Frankincense Trail. Merchants used this ancient trade route—also called the Incense Trail—for transporting frankincense, myrrh, precious gems, gold, and other luxury goods. Originating at the southern tip of the Arabian Peninsula, the route wound its way northward through modern-day Saudi Arabia, Jordan, and Israel, and then on to Lebanon and Syria. Her journey to Jerusalem would have taken several months.

What could have compelled such a powerful and wealthy queen to make this fifteen-hundred-mile journey? Besides facing harsh desert conditions, her royal caravan would have been exposed to thieves and raiders as well as taxation by various tribal groups along the route. Potential local conflicts could have quickly shut down the route. It wouldn't have been an easy trip even for a confident and powerful queen.

By her own telling, the Queen of Sheba's legendary journey was prompted by curiosity. She needed to see for herself whether the tales of Solomon's wealth and wisdom were true. She may also have been on a mission to protect her own trade routes from the naval force Solomon had developed (1 Kings 9:26-28).

When she arrived, she peppered Israel's king with hard questions to test him. The word for "hard questions" is *hidot*, which refers to riddles, difficult challenges, or deep questions, mysterious matters that only wisdom can comprehend. Solomon dazzled the queen by answering everything she threw at him. And she returned the favor by dazzling him with all the gifts she had brought—a vast horde of spices, gems, and gold.

The Queen of Sheba's own wisdom shone through when she attributed the source of Solomon's wealth and wisdom not to the king himself but to the loving God he followed. She praised this God for placing a wise king on the throne, whose purpose would not merely be to amass power but to maintain justice and righteousness.

THE QUEEN OF SHEBA'S *Legacy* IN SCRIPTURE

READ

1 Kings 10:1-13

- How might the Queen of Sheba, ruler of a land far from Israel, have heard about Solomon?

- What does it mean that Solomon was famous for "his relationship to the LORD" (1 Kings 10:1)?

- Choose several words that you think describe this queen.

- What questions do you think the Queen of Sheba might have asked Solomon? Think of questions you would ask Solomon if you could.

- How would you define wisdom? Describe someone you know who is truly wise. What are their characteristics?

- Why is wisdom important? Where could you go to find wisdom?

OUR *Connection* TO THE QUEEN OF SHEBA

Once again, a Gentile woman—an outsider—played a key role in Israel's story. Though she had enormous wealth, her longing for wisdom compelled her to leave the comforts of her own land to travel across vast deserts in search of the truth. Her story is later echoed in Isaiah 60:6, which mentions Sheba and pictures foreign nations streaming into God's kingdom.

- Read Matthew 2:1-12. What does this story of the Magi who visited Jesus have in common with the story of the Queen of Sheba?

- In Matthew 12:42, Jesus says the Queen of the South (of Sheba) will testify against his generation. What do you think that means in terms of her recognition of greatness and of God's character?

- What questions are on your heart right now that you need to bring to God? What are you willing to do to obtain wisdom?

Lord, I need wisdom to make right decisions but also simply to live well. Remind me that you have promised wisdom to any who ask, and that you don't give grudgingly or with a tight fist but with an open and generous hand.

WEEK 27

JEZEBEL

"WHERE IS THE PRINCE?" A PHRASE ASSOCIATED WITH BAAL WORSHIP OR, BASED ON HEBREW WORDPLAY, "NOT EXALTED"

Her Story

A queen of Israel known for her extreme wickedness, Jezebel expanded the worship of Baal in Israel.

There was never anyone like Ahab, who sold himself to do evil in the eyes of the Lord, urged on by Jezebel his wife. 1 KINGS 21:25

READ

1 Kings 16:29-33; 18:1-19:2; 21:1-25; 2 Kings 9

Who WAS SHE?

Jezebel was married to Israel's King Ahab, the king whose name conjures images of extreme evil. He was known as one of Israel's wickedest kings, with his queen close behind. Her machinations to gain Naboth's vineyard for her whiny, covetous husband included rigging false testimony to force a death sentence on an innocent man. The coming judgment the prophet Elijah had spoken against the queen and the king then came cascading down on their heads.

A *Closer Look* AT JEZEBEL'S STORY

HER STORY TOOK PLACE AROUND 874–841 BC.

How we love villains! Jezebel's name persists even into the twenty-first century, one of the few women in the Bible who seems entirely corrupt. Where did she come from?

First, a little background story. After Solomon's death, the tribes of Israel divided in two, with ten tribes professing loyalty to Israel in the north and three tribes (Judah, Benjamin, and Levi) remaining in Judah in the south. Note that Levi, which never received a tribal inheritance of land, wasn't considered part of the twelve tribes but had been set apart to perform religious duties on behalf of the entire people.

The Phoenician princess Jezebel came onto the scene when she married Ahab, the son of Omri, who was Israel's sixth and worst king. Under his pagan wife's influence, Ahab surpassed even his father in wickedness.

One of the first things we learn about Jezebel is her determination to spread Baal worship by slaughtering God's prophets and then replacing them with 850 prophets of the Canaanite deities Baal and Asherah. Baal (meaning "lord" or "master") was a Canaanite storm and fertility god, widely worshiped and called by various names, depending on the location. Baal Melqart may have been the particular manifestation Jezebel worshiped.

Influenced by his wife, King Ahab built a temple to Baal, thus spreading Baal worship alongside the worship of Israel's God, Yahweh. That's where Elijah came in—to pronounce judgment on Ahab's apostasy and idolatry.

The famous scene on Mount Carmel, where Elijah challenged his onlookers to stop wavering between two opinions, pitted the fiery prophet against Jezebel's 850 frantic, self-mutilating prophets. It's hard to read the story without chuckling over Elijah's sarcastic barbs when Baal failed the contest. But Jezebel never saw the humor. After learning of the demise of her prophets, she threatened Elijah, saying, "May the gods deal with me, be it ever so severely, if by this time tomorrow I do not make your life like that of one of them" (1 Kings 19:2). Though it took a few years, God did deal severely, not with Elijah, but with both Jezebel and Ahab after they falsely accused and executed a man named Naboth so the king could confiscate his beautiful vineyard.

Confronting Ahab afterward, Elijah thundered, "'In the place where dogs licked up Naboth's blood, dogs will lick up your blood—yes, yours!' . . . And also concerning Jezebel the LORD says: 'Dogs will devour Jezebel by the wall of Jezreel'" (1 Kings 21:19, 23).

It happened just as Elijah had foretold. After Ahab's death, while Jezebel was residing in her palace at Jezreel, a usurper arrived, but not before slaying her son on the vineyard that had formerly belonged to Naboth. Riding on to the palace, he urged Jezebel's servants to cast her down from a window where she stood taunting him. Trampled by horses and eaten by dogs, the evil and murderous queen, who had issued so many vile threats, finally had nothing at all to say.

JEZEBEL'S *Legacy* IN SCRIPTURE

READ

1 Kings 16:29-33; 18:3-4; 19:1-2; 21:1-25

- What kind of relationship did Jezebel have with her husband, Ahab?

- As queen, how did Jezebel treat her subjects?

- Jezebel broke a number of civil and moral laws in order to gain Naboth's vineyard for Ahab. What does this tell you about her understanding of her position and power?

- What character traits do you see in Jezebel based on these passages? What might have caused her to become so evil?

READ
2 Kings 9:30-37

- Why would Scripture record that Jezebel prepared for Jehu's arrival by putting on eye makeup and arranging her hair? Is this significant? Why or why not?

- How do you feel about Jezebel's death? In general, do you like to see people getting what they deserve? What is the difference between justice and revenge?

OUR *Connection* TO JEZEBEL

Jezebel was a devoutly religious woman who believed that Baal could deliver prosperity to Israel. Manipulative, immoral, and corrupt, she abused her power to get her own way. Even after Elijah's God had dramatically defeated Baal at Mount Carmel, she rigidly clung to her beliefs.

Unfortunately, in some segments of the church today, Jezebel's story has been weaponized and used against women, projected onto them simply because they have spoken or acted in a way that some in the church dislike. This is especially true of women who challenge corrupt leadership within the church.

- Jezebel's wickedness was rooted in idolatry and in her zeal to spread it. In what ways do you recognize idolatry, both subtle and overt, at work in our world today?

- What does the lopsided struggle between Elijah and the 850 false prophets say about the nature of true spiritual power?

God of justice and mercy, the evil in these stories is easy to see. But that isn't always true. Give me spiritual eyes to see what is good and what is not. Then help me to live in a way that reflects justice but also mercy.

WEEK 28

THE WIDOW OF ZAREPHATH

Her Story

This widow displayed remarkable hospitality by generously sharing the last of her food with the prophet Elisha. She needed a miracle to keep herself and her son from starving.

She went away and did as Elijah had told her. So there was food every day for Elijah and for the woman and her family. 1 KINGS 17:15

READ

1 Kings 17; Luke 4:25–26

Who WAS SHE?

On the verge of starvation, this widow was gathering sticks for a fire so that she could prepare a last meal for herself and her son when she encountered a man with what felt like an impossible request: "Bring me, please, a piece of bread" (1 Kings

17:11). Did she believe his declaration that the food—sparse as it was—would be miraculously enough? Or did she think it no longer mattered whether she died today or tomorrow? Why not share whatever they had? Little did she know her gift of hospitality would bring with it the gift of life.

A *Closer Look* AT THE WIDOW OF ZAREPHATH'S STORY

HER STORY TOOK PLACE AROUND 870–850 BC.

North of Jezreel, where Jezebel's story unfolded, lived an impoverished Phoenician woman. She resided in Zarephath, just south of Sidon, a region governed by Jezebel's priest/king father, an avid devotee of Baal. Though Baal's followers touted him as a storm god, there hadn't been a single drop of rain for some time.

While the Canaanite god had his eye on the sky, Elijah's God had his eye on the sparrow, which is why he told the prophet to head north. He had chosen a widow, weakened by poverty and hunger, to become his sturdy instrument, a source of refuge for Elijah, for she would feed him in a time of famine.

Not long before, Elijah had confronted Israel's king with the sin of idolatry, saying to Ahab, "As the LORD, the God of Israel, lives, whom I serve, there will be neither dew nor rain in the next few years except at my word" (1 Kings 17:1). Then Elijah hid out in the wilderness, where God miraculously sustained him, feeding him meat twice a day. That detail, like most details in the Bible, is important because people in that time rarely ate meat. Even the king's table served meat just once a day. By contrast, Elijah, sitting at the divine King's table, ate meat twice a day! Then, when the brook he drank from dried up, God told him to seek out the widow at once.

How remarkable that her radical act of hospitality—feeding the prophet the last of her bread—unleashed an even more radical act of hospitality on God's part! For her jar of flour and her jug of oil never ran out, and there was always enough food to sustain her son, herself, and the prophet.

But why a foreign widow when so many in Israel were suffering? The message would have been clear to the Israelites.

An outsider, someone not considered one of God's chosen people, was more open to God than they were, which is why he served justice to them and food to her.

In Luke 4:25-26, Jesus called attention to her story. Speaking to people in Nazareth, he foretold yet another refusal on the part of God's people: their failure to trust in him. He also forecast what would happen after his death. Because of Israel's unbelief, God's blessings would spread quickly to the Gentiles.

The text never explores Elijah's feelings about God's way of providing for him. A starving Phoenician widow and her son, who lived by Jezebel's hometown, might have seemed like anything but provision. He, too, had to exercise faith. But as they both did so, the flour and the oil kept multiplying. Enough—and more than enough!

THE WIDOW OF ZAREPHATH'S *Legacy* IN SCRIPTURE

READ

1 Kings 17:7-24

- Compare Luke 4:25–26 with 1 Kings 17:9. What is going on in these verses? Why would God choose a pagan widow rather than one of the widows of Israel?

- This woman is honest with Elijah about her lack of food. Why?

- What does Elijah say that perhaps convinces her to obey? What could this tell you about her knowledge of the God of Israel?

- Why would God use a destitute woman to help Elijah rather than someone who had more to share? What is God doing here?

- Where does the widow place the blame for her son's death? Why do you think she brings up her past sin?

- The last words from the widow are a declaration of faith. Why do you think it took the resurrection of her son for her to believe?

OUR *Connection* TO THE WIDOW OF ZAREPHATH

Later in her story, the widow encountered Elijah again. This time she was not starving but grieving, for her son had fallen ill and died. Blaming herself for some hidden sin, she railed at the prophet, and he responded by praying. When her son revived, she witnessed the first resurrection in the Bible. Through the remarkable events of her life, God shaped a story of grace in a time of judgment.

- What does the widow's story reveal about God?

- How do you make sense of difficult situations in your own life? How has prayer transformed the circumstances or your attitude toward God, yourself, and others?

- Modern readers often flinch at the word *judgment* but warm to the word *justice*. The Hebrew word *mishpat* can be translated as "justice" or "judgment." How would your understanding of God and the Bible change if you were to substitute the word *judgment* for *justice* as you read Scripture (e.g., Exodus 6:6; Isaiah 26:9; Psalm 9:7–8)?

God of surprises, sometimes the way you work and the people you use astonishes us, not just in Bible times but also today. Give us divine understanding and willing acceptance of your perfect ways and wisdom, now and always.

WEEK 29

THE SHUNAMMITE WOMAN

Her Story

Another one of Scripture's unnamed women, she welcomed the prophet Elisha into her home, even creating a special place for him to rest when his travels took him through her town.

She said to her husband, "I know that this man who often comes our way is a holy man of God. Let's make a small room on the roof .... Then he can stay here whenever he comes to us." 2 KINGS 4:9-10

READ

2 Kings 4:8-37; 8:1-6

Who WAS SHE?

It's hard not to feel this woman's anguish, watching as her beloved son dies in her arms. A son she had not asked for—but may secretly have longed for—had been miraculously given to her and then suddenly snatched away. Rather than accept the obvious, concluding that nothing more could be done for him, she rushed to the prophet, brushing his assistant aside and insisting Elisha go to her son. Only through faith, persistence, divine timing, and the grace of God did her son come back to life, enabling her to hold him in her arms once again.

A *Closer Look* AT THE SHUNAMMITE WOMAN'S STORY

HER STORY TOOK PLACE AROUND 850–835 BC.

In Shunem, a town not five miles from Jezreel, there lived a rich woman who went out of her way to care for Elisha, the prophet who succeeded Elijah. Her cooking was so good and her hospitality so gracious that the prophet stopped by whenever he was in the area.

One day she asked her husband if they could build a small addition on the roof of their home to house the prophet whenever he visited. Grateful for her hospitality, Elisha asked if he might repay her by putting in a good word to the king on her behalf. But she demurred, saying that she had "a home among [her] own people" (2 Kings 4:13), meaning she was secure and needed nothing.

But when Elisha's servant Gehazi suggested that the childless woman might long for a son, Elisha called for her again. As she stood in the doorway, he prophesied: "About this time next year . . . you will hold a son in your arms" (2 Kings 4:16). Her story in that moment echoes the story of the biblical matriarch Sarah, who had also stood at a doorway (the entrance to her tent when an angelic visitor told her husband Abraham that "about this time next year . . . Sarah your wife will have a son" (Genesis 18:10).

Both women were married to old men. Both were childless. Both showed hospitality. Neither fully believed the miraculous promise that had been spoken.

Nevertheless, both delivered a son a year later. Both also nearly lost their sons—Isaac when Abraham was going to sacrifice him and the Shunammite woman's son when he became ill.

Sometime after the young boy's resurrection, Elisha warned the Shunammite woman to leave the area to escape a seven-year famine. Because she acted on his warning, God preserved and then greatly blessed her family. Seven years later, on her return, she went to the king to request that her land be given back to her. Before she even had a chance to ask, she ran into Gehazi, who just happened to be telling the king about how Elisha had healed her son. The king not only decreed that her land be returned but that she receive all the income it had produced in her seven-year absence, income that would otherwise have belonged to whomever had been farming it during that time.

To be deprived of food your own hands had planted was considered a great punishment. But to eat food that someone else had planted? Everyone in Israel knew that was a wonderful blessing. Wasn't that precisely how God had cared for his people when they first entered the land of Canaan (Deuteronomy 6:10-11)?

The Shunammite woman's story, unfolding more than a thousand years after Sarah's, would have comforted the Israelites, reinvigorating their trust in God. Like an exquisitely painted miniature, her life portrayed not only God's past faithfulness but the way he was still working to fulfill the ancient covenant promise.[8]

8 For a more complete treatment of her story, see Frymer-Kensky, *Reading the Women of the Bible*, 64–73.

THE SHUNAMMITE WOMAN'S *Legacy* IN SCRIPTURE

READ

2 Kings 4:8-37

- What caused this woman to go out of her way to make Elisha comfortable in her home?

- How did the Shunammite woman answer when asked what could be done for her in response to her hospitality? What did she mean? Compare 2 Kings 4:16 and 4:28.

- The woman responded in an unusual way when her son died. Why would she act as she did, and what was she hoping to accomplish?

- What important similarities do you see between this story and the similar one in 1 Kings 17:19–24? What does it reveal about God that he decided to resurrect these two boys when there were most likely other mothers at the same time who lost their sons?

- What admirable qualities of the Shunammite woman might you imitate?

OUR *Connection* TO THE SHUNAMMITE WOMAN

Unlike other childless women whose stories are told in Scripture, the Shunammite woman never asked for a son. Yet once she had him, she did whatever was necessary to keep him. Even when her faith was tested, she didn't dissolve into despair but took action, rushing to Mount Carmel and insisting that Elisha himself intercede for her boy. Hers is a story of generosity, faith, tenacity, and answered prayer.

- Details are always important in the Bible. In this case, note the detail of standing in the doorway (2 Kings 4:15). Doorways, doorposts, thresholds, or gateways in Scripture can be symbolic places where divine encounters, promises, and transformations occur. Describe a symbolic doorway in your own life and its significance to you.

- What might it look like to make more space in your life for God as this woman did when she built a room for Elisha?

Lord, help me to have the kind of generosity and faith that this woman had, responding quickly to opportunities you give me to help others. Whenever my faith is weak, remind me of her story.

WEEK 30

ATHALIAH

"THE LORD IS GREAT"

Her Story

The only queen of Judah, she wielded death in one hand and idolatry in the other.

When Athaliah the mother of Ahaziah saw that her son was dead, she proceeded to destroy the whole royal family. 2 KINGS 11:1

JEHOSHEBA

"GOD IS MY OATH"

Her Story

She was a godly princess, married to the high priest in Jerusalem. With quick thinking and courageous actions, she saved the life of the rightful king of Judah, preserving the lineage from which the Messiah would come.

But Jehosheba ... took Joash son of Ahaziah and stole him away from among the royal princes, who were about to be murdered. 2 KINGS 11:2

READ

2 Kings 11; 2 Chronicles 22; 23:11-21

Who WERE THEY?

When Athaliah heard that her son Ahaziah, king of Judah, had been killed by Jehu, the king of Israel, she went on a killing spree, ordering the deaths of every single grandson lest any inherit the throne. In the confusion following Ahaziah's sudden death, she failed to realize that her ruthless order hadn't been completely carried out. Her plans were foiled by Jehosheba, another member of the royal family. Though Athaliah became queen of Judah, Jehosheba acted quickly to save the young prince and then hide him in the temple for six years before bringing him out and proclaiming him king.

A *Closer Look* AT ATHALIAH'S AND JEHOSHEBA'S STORIES

THEIR STORIES TOOK PLACE AROUND BETWEEN 841–835 BC.

Though Elijah had killed 850 false prophets during the reign of Ahab and Jezebel, the evil queen didn't meet a violent end until a man named Jehu entered the scene. In addition to causing Jezebel's death, he wiped out all of Ahab's male descendants and then claimed the throne of the Northern Kingdom of Israel for himself. One of his victims was Ahaziah, king of the Southern Kingdom of Judah. He was Ahab and Jezebel's grandson.

Though the Bible depicts Ahaziah as an evil king (2 Kings 8:25-27), his mother Athaliah surpassed his wickedness. The Bible identifies her as the daughter of Ahab. Whether she was Jezebel's daughter or only her stepdaughter, their wicked hearts seemed to beat as one.

To form a closer political alliance between the Northern Kingdom and the Southern Kingdom, Ahab had arranged for his daughter Athaliah to marry Jehoram, the king of

Judah. While Ahab and Jezebel imported Baal worship into the Northern Kingdom, Athaliah's husband, Jehoram, began spreading it in the Southern Kingdom.

After King Jehoram's death, their son Ahaziah became the king of Judah, but only for one year. After his murder (2 Kings 9:27–29), his mother, Athaliah, usurped the throne. Determined to wipe out the Davidic dynasty to secure her rule, she proceeded to destroy the royal family, killing even her own grandsons.

But one tiny heir escaped. A compassionate, courageous, and quick-witted aunt spirited baby Joash away. The aunt, Jehosheba, married to the high priest Jehoiada and described as Ahaziah's sister, may have been Queen Athaliah's stepdaughter rather than her daughter. With her husband's help, Princess Jehosheba sheltered Joash in the temple for six years. Imagine what it must have cost her to hide the rightful king under the nose of his murderous grandmother.

Queen Athaliah, the only woman ever to rule Judah, reigned for six years. In the seventh year, Jehosheba's husband, the high priest Jehoiada, overthrew her and then executed her so that young Joash could ascend to the throne.

God had promised a Messiah who would come from the tribe of Judah, specifically from David's line. Though the promise had nearly been extinguished, a woman who was a close relative of an evil queen helped preserve it. Athaliah acted like a female pharaoh, murdering children to secure her power, while Princess Jehosheba acted like Pharaoh's daughter, saving a baby who would one day lead the nation. With compassion and courage, Jehosheba preserved the life of a child who would carry on the line of David, from whom Jesus, the Messiah, would be born.

ATHALIAH'S AND JEHOSHEBA'S *Legacy* IN SCRIPTURE

READ

2 Kings 11

- Contrast the acts of these two women. Now contrast what motivated each of them and what they were hoping to accomplish.

- The number of deaths within God's chosen people, recorded in 2 Kings 10-11, is remarkable and horrifying. What does this say about the nation's spiritual condition at the time?

- What are the chances that Jehosheba knew her actions preserved the line of the Messiah? Why was this lineage important?

- Why would Jehosheba choose the temple as a hiding place for young Joash? Where else could she have hidden him?

- How was God involved in these events? Do you think Satan also played a part?

- Have you ever had a part in thwarting the devil's plan?

- What about Jehosheba is worth emulating? What circumstances in your life require you to have her characteristics?

OUR *Connection* TO ATHALIAH AND JEHOSHEBA

The prophet Micah exhorted his people, saying,

> He has shown you, O mortal, what is good.
> And what does the LORD require of you?
> To act justly and to love mercy
> and to walk humbly with your God (Micah 6:8).

Athaliah and Jehosheba stand at opposite ends of the spectrum. Family ties, nationality, and ethnicity are circumstantial. Who we will become is shaped by whom we will obey.

The Bible rarely supplies a description of a character's inner life, instead defining people in terms of their words and actions. By doing so, it invites us to slow down and carefully ponder the narrative. Spend five minutes imagining you are Jehosheba. What motivates you to save the child's life? How do you feel as you endure the stress of hiding him for six years? What are your thoughts as your husband fights to put Joash on the throne?

Lord, you still reign no matter what is happening here on earth. Help me to have the wisdom and courage to stand for what is right in a world that sometimes seems as dark as the days of Jehosheba.

WEEK 31

HULDAH

"WEASEL" OR "MOLE"

Her Story

During a time of tremendous apostasy in the kingdom of Judah, she prophesied disaster.

[Huldah] said to them . . . " 'This is what the LORD says: I am going to bring disaster on this place and its people.' " 2 KINGS 22:15-16

READ

2 Kings 22:1-23:30; 2 Chronicles 34

Who WAS SHE?

King Josiah's emissaries came to the prophet Huldah, asking her to verify dire words of judgment written in the newly discovered book of the law. Harsh words tumbled from Huldah's lips, confirming that catastrophe was coming for Judah because of its idolatry. She had watched as her people bowed down to idols and sacrificed their children on pagan altars. Now, she foretold a reckoning that would bring death and ruin. But for the king she prophesied mercy. Because he had repented the moment he read the scroll, Judah's judgment would not arrive until after his death.

A *Closer Look* AT HULDAH'S STORY

HER STORY TOOK PLACE AROUND 622 BC.

Josiah was the sixteenth king of Judah and one of the few who "did what was right in the eyes of the LORD" (2 Kings 22:2). He ascended the throne as an eight-year-old. At the age of twenty, he began purging the Southern Kingdom from idolatry. And how Judah needed it!

Three hundred years earlier, the Queen of Sheba had beheld Solomon's glorious temple. If she could have time-traveled forward to Huldah's day, she would have been shocked at its desecration. Solomon had dedicated the Eden-like structure, with its beautiful garden of Eden imagery—palm trees, pomegranates, cherubim, and menorahs to symbolize the tree of life (Exodus 25:31–40; 1 Kings 6:23–35)—to the one God of Israel. Now, it was chock-full of idols.

There were pagan altars on the roof, statues of horses and chariots for sun worship, a wooden Asherah pole carved in the image of the Canaanite goddess, articles for Baal worship, and rooms reserved for male prostitutes to promote fertility worship. But the most vile, despicable pollution of this holy space and city, where God had promised to dwell, took place on altars dedicated to child sacrifice. Just two years prior to Josiah's reign, the evil king Manasseh had ruled. He sacrificed his own children in the Valley of Hinnom, just outside Jerusalem's walls. He also practiced witchcraft and consulted spiritists (2 Chronicles 33:6). This place would later be known as Gehenna, often translated as "hell" in English Bibles.

How far God's people had fallen! After their Egyptian captivity, they had been invited into the promised land as into a new Eden. The temple would become the epicenter, a connecting point between heaven and earth. But by Josiah's day it had become a hell on earth.

This is essential background for understanding the prophet Huldah's role in the story. After living through at least part of Manasseh's corrupt fifty-five-year reign, she must have been relieved and heartened by Josiah's early reforms.

Though women were usually barred from public positions in government and religion, both women and men could be prophets. Named female prophets include

Huldah, Miriam (Exodus 15:20), Deborah (Judges 4:4), Isaiah's wife (Isaiah 8:3), and Anna (Luke 2:36).

Though the prophet Jeremiah was active at the time, the king's counselors went straight to Huldah after they discovered the book of the law (probably the core of the book of Deuteronomy) in the temple. If the king hoped its severe warnings against idolatry could be averted, Huldah disappointed him, saying, "'This is what the LORD says: I am going to bring disaster on this place and its people, according to everything written in the book the king of Judah has read'" (2 Kings 22:16). But then God spoke a softer word through her, assuring the good King Josiah that because he had torn his robes and wept in God's presence, he would not live to see the disaster himself.

Huldah's faithful rendering of God's intentions sparked both a call to repentance and one of the greatest religious reforms in history. What's more, her validation of the text was the first recorded act in a process that would eventually result in the authoritative written canon of the Bible.

Huldah's *Legacy* in Scripture

READ

2 Kings 22:8-20

- What significance is there in the fact that the law of God had been lost *in his temple*? What does this tell you about the spiritual condition of Judah?

- Describe Josiah's reaction. Why would he react in such a way?

- Why might Josiah go to an unknown female prophet instead of other more notable—and male—prophets of the time, such as Jeremiah?

- Explain what this story teaches us about God's:

  Justice

  Mercy

  Grace

  Forgiveness

- Explore how Huldah responded to her difficult task. What can she teach you?

OUR *Connection* TO HULDAH

Huldah must have been a known quantity—respected for her authority, understanding, and connection to God—because the king and his men consulted her when it seemed that the nation stood on a knife-edge as a result of its idolatry and ignorance of God's Word. Sadly, after Josiah's reforms, subsequent kings reversed course, leading the people astray once again. In 586 BC, the judgment Huldah had earlier confirmed finally arrived when Babylon conquered Judah and carried many of its people into exile.

- Have you ever consulted someone you thought was wise and close to God, as Josiah did with Huldah? Why and when is it important to do so?

- In what ways has God spoken personally to you? How have you learned over the course of your life to hear him more clearly?

- How is it possible to discern whether someone possesses a true prophetic voice?

Lord, how many of my own sins deserve your judgment!
I take a moment now to examine myself and repent.
Thank you that because of Jesus' life, death, and
resurrection, I can receive your grace and redemption.
I pray that you purify me along with your church.

WEEK 32

ESTHER

HER NAME MAY DERIVE FROM *ISHTAR,* THE BABYLONIAN GODDESS OF LOVE, OR FROM THE PERSIAN WORD FOR "STAR." HER HEBREW NAME, *HADASSAH,* MEANS "MYRTLE."

Her Story

Esther's beauty gained her the dubious privilege of joining Xerxes' harem of women after Queen Vashti disobeyed the king's order.

Now the king was attracted to Esther more than to any of the other women, and she won his favor and approval more than any of the other virgins. So he set a royal crown on her head and made her queen. ESTHER 2:17

READ

Esther 1-10

Who WAS SHE?

Esther's story is hardly romantic. She and her cousin Mordecai were living in Persia as exiles when King Xerxes' officials launched an empire-wide beauty pageant to find a new queen for the king. Esther's beauty soon landed her in the king's harem. When her turn with the king came, Xerxes was so smitten with Esther that he married her. Queen though she was, Esther was also an orphan and a secret Jew, living as an alien in a foreign land after her people had earlier been carried off to Babylon. When faced with the threat of a Jewish genocide, she acted not as a vacuous beauty queen but as a forceful and faithful woman of God.

A Closer Look AT ESTHER'S STORY

HER STORY TOOK PLACE AROUND 480–465 BC.

Because of its persistent apostasy, the Northern Kingdom of Israel, over which Ahab and Jezebel had ruled, fell to Assyria in 722 BC. In the Southern Kingdom, despite Josiah's reforms and Huldah's prophetic ministry, Judah continued to rebel against God and was overrun by Babylon in 586 BC. Judgment fell like a hammer when King Nebuchadnezzar destroyed Solomon's magnificent temple and dragged many into captivity. Then, in 539 BC, Cyrus of Persia overran Babylon. The orphaned Esther and her cousin Mordecai were Jewish exiles living in the vast Persian Empire. Both belonged to the tribe of Benjamin, which had also been King Saul's tribe.

God is never directly mentioned in the book of Esther.[9] When Esther's story unfolded, Xerxes I reigned over Persia. The Greek historian Herodotus depicted him as ambitious, arrogant, impulsive, emotionally indulgent, and prone to rage. Though Xerxes probably had many wives and concubines, Esther replaced the disobedient Queen Vashti as his chief wife.

There are several comic notes and reversals throughout Esther's wonderful story, which begins and ends with a banquet. In between, there are three additional banquets, and each banquet marks a turning point in the story.

The chief villain in the story was a man by the name of Haman, an Agagite. Since Agag was an Amalekite king, the implication is that Haman was also an Amalekite. A nomadic desert tribe, the Amalekites

9 Protestant translations of the Bible include a shorter version of the book of Esther because they are based on the Hebrew Masoretic text, while Roman Catholic and various Orthodox translations include the longer version, which does mention God, because they are based on the Greek Septuagint version.

descended from Rebekah's son Esau. The first to attack the Israelites after their escape from Egypt, they were also the first to suffer defeat at the hand of the former slaves (Exodus 17:8-16). Afterward, God told Moses, "Write this on a scroll as something to be remembered and make sure that Joshua hears it, because I will completely blot out the name of Amalek from under heaven" (Exodus 17:14). Because of their persistent hostility toward Israel, the Amalekites came to symbolize all the powers of the world that were arrayed against God's people.

Early in his reign, Israel's first king, Saul, disobeyed God's command to wipe out the Amalekites. Instead he spared the life of King Agag (1 Samuel 15). For his disobedience, God rejected him as king. It would be left to two other Benjaminites—Esther and Mordecai—to finish the job several hundred years later. How remarkable that God's promise to defeat Israel's archenemy was finally fulfilled, not when his people were on top of the world, living comfortably in their own land, but in the middle of exile, precisely at the time when they would have felt their weakest and most vulnerable!

Gifted with extraordinary beauty, Esther displayed wisdom, courage, persuasion, and perfect timing to reverse a genocidal decree and preserve the Jewish nation in exile. Instead of trying to save her own life, she listened to Mordecai's warning: "Do not think that because you are in the king's house you alone of all the Jews will escape. For if you remain silent at this time, relief and deliverance for the Jews will arise from another place, but you and your father's family will perish. And who knows but that you have come to your royal position for such a time as this?" (Esther 4:12-14).

ESTHER'S *Legacy* IN SCRIPTURE

READ

Esther 3:12-4:17

- Let's begin at the beginning. Why would Queen Vashti refuse the commands of King Xerxes?

- On entering the harem, Esther concealed her Jewish roots. Why?

- Describe Esther's character. Was she a willing participant in these events, or was she forced? (Keep in mind the honor, wealth, and luxurious life available to her as part of a king's harem.)

- What might have compelled Esther to act as she did? Include Esther 4:12-14 in your answer.

- What surprises you about the fact that God's name is never mentioned in the book of Esther? Where, if anywhere, do you see God at work despite the absence of his name?

- Write about what might have happened if Esther had done nothing.

OUR *Connection* TO ESTHER

What must it have been like for the orphaned Esther to grow up as an exile, a member of a minority group that had been forcibly removed from their country? How might she have felt when she was dragged into the king's harem, subjected to a year of beauty treatments and then forced to marry him? Instead of shrinking back in hopes of saving her own life and preserving her exalted position, she took a dangerous risk. Before doing so, she asked Mordecai to gather the Jews and join her for a three-day fast. Only then did she put her plan into motion.

- Esther's position was no accident, and neither is yours. How might God want you to use the influence he's given you where he has you right now?

- What does the book of Esther reveal about our call to live faithfully in a hostile culture?

- How might fasting with other believers provide wisdom and courage for facing life's challenges?

God, thank you for an example like Esther, a woman with remarkable courage. You might not ask me to go before a king and risk death, but I trust that you will shape my heart to be more like hers.

WEEK 33

THE WOMAN OF PROVERBS 31

Her Story

The woman of Proverbs 31 does it all. But above and beyond her outward achievements lies an inner reverence for the Lord, one that animates her life.

"Many women do noble things, but you surpass them all." … a woman who fears the Lord is to be praised. PROVERBS 31:29-30

READ

Proverbs 8; 9:13–18; 31:10–31

Who WAS SHE?

Verse by verse, Proverbs 31 praises a woman and her accomplishments, the sum of which seem more than any one woman could perform, even in a lifetime. Perhaps these verses aren't meant to portray a particular woman but many different women who use their wisdom and gifts to support their families and help others. More important than their competence and hard work is the way they revere and respect the God they serve.

A *Closer Look* AT THE PROVERBS 31 WOMAN'S STORY

Full of short, poetic sayings, the book of Proverbs offers practical advice for how to live the best life possible by cultivating wisdom—by becoming skilled in doing what is right. Two figurative characters, Lady Folly and Lady Wisdom, cry out to any who will listen. One voice leads to life and the other to death.

Proverbs pictures Lady Folly as an empty-minded and unruly woman, sitting on her doorstep and calling out:

> "Let all who are simple come to my
> house!" . . .
> But little do they know that the dead
> are there,
> that her guests are deep in the realm
> of the dead (Proverbs 9:16, 18).

In Proverbs 8, a long passage that is surely the most beautiful and profound description of wisdom ever written, Lady Wisdom also calls out, but she speaks of another way:

> "Choose my instruction instead of silver,
> knowledge rather than choice gold,
> for wisdom is more precious than rubies,
> and nothing you desire can compare
> with her" (Proverbs 8:10-11).

Proverbs 31 forms the capstone of the entire book, offering an animated view of what a life of wisdom looks like and what it can produce. The woman portrayed here is drawn in ideal, almost superhuman terms. She not only provides for her own household, but her fruitfulness overflows to the poor and needy.

Most households in Israel would have consisted of parents, grandparents, adult sons and their families, unmarried sisters, possibly a widow with her children, and a few servants. Picture an average of perhaps twelve people living together.[10] The wealthy woman portrayed here probably had a much larger household.

As the ideal wife, the Proverbs 31 woman had amazing capabilities. She knew how to care for children, thresh and grind grain, knead and bake bread, spin and weave wool, and make clothing for her household. Though most women spent their days working at home or close to

10 Miriam Feinberg Vamosh, *Women at the Time of the Bible* (Nashville: Abingdon Press, 2007), 5.

home, they also worked in the fields and cared for the flocks. When the men went off to war, they had to cover every possible task to keep their household going. The Proverbs 31 woman went beyond all this by buying a field, planting a vineyard, and engaging in profitable trade.

But the secret of this ideal woman's success, which extended beyond the home, was not her capabilities nor her commitment to working from morning to night. The secret was that she feared the Lord, that she held him in awe, because "the fear of the LORD is the beginning of wisdom" (Proverbs 9:10) and "[wisdom] is a tree of life" (Proverbs 3:18).

Though this portrait of the ideal wife has sometimes been twisted to browbeat and shame women, the real purpose of Proverbs 31 is the opposite. It is meant to encourage all of us—whether male or female—to embrace wisdom so that we can become the kind of people whose lives teem with God's blessings and overflow to others.

THE PROVERBS 31 WOMAN'S *Legacy* IN SCRIPTURE

READ

Proverbs 31:10-31

- Does the writer of Proverbs 31 focus more on the woman's character or actions—or both? How does one play into the other?

- Explore the kind of relationship this woman had with her husband, reflecting on each verse where he's mentioned.

- Why is this woman able to "laugh at the days to come" (Proverbs 31:25)?

- Does Proverbs 31:30 inspire you or make you uneasy? Explain why. If you're finding your priorities are out of order, what will you do?

- Choose just one verse or phrase from this chapter, and explain why that particular truth speaks to you and your life today.

- Write your own simple, contemporary version of Proverbs 31.

OUR *Connection* TO THE WOMAN OF PROVERBS 31

How beautiful that the Bible personifies wisdom as a woman! Listen to these words from the lips of Lady Wisdom:

> "To fear the LORD is to hate evil;
>   I hate pride and arrogance,
>   evil behavior and perverse speech.
> Counsel and sound judgment are mine;
>   I have insight, I have power.
> By me kings reign
>   and rulers issue decrees that are just;
> by me princes govern,
>   and nobles—all who rule on earth.
> I love those who love me,
>   and those who seek me find me.
> With me are riches and honor,
>   enduring wealth and prosperity . . . .
>   and [I make] their treasuries full" (Proverbs 8:13-18, 21).

- Spend a few moments picturing Lady Wisdom addressing you. Ask the Holy Spirit to bring her words to life as you meditate on this image. What might it mean to fear the Lord, hating every trace of pride, arrogance, and perverse speech in your life? What kind of power does wisdom have?

- Read through Proverbs 8 slowly and meditatively, asking God to highlight the passages that he particularly wants to bring to your attention. What stands out? How can you respond?

All-wise God, help me to see from these words how to gain wisdom so that it will mold the way I live. You are the source of wisdom, and you've promised it to all who ask. I'm asking. Teach me wisdom as I meditate on these words.

WEEK 34

THE SHULAMMITE WOMAN

Her Story

The lovely and desirable Shulammite woman longs for her beloved, expressing deep devotion and joy in their mutual love.

Let him kiss me with the kisses of his mouth—
for your love is more delightful than wine. SONG OF SONGS 1:2

READ

Song of Songs 1-8

Who WAS SHE?

The Shulammite woman appears throughout the eight chapters of Song of Songs but is named only in Song of Songs 6:13. She both desired and was desired by her lover.

Their physical attraction as well as their individual character qualities drew them together. The book celebrates the love and intimacy between a husband and wife but also illustrates the relationship of Christ with his bride, the church (Ephesians 5:25-27).

A *Closer Look* AT THE SHULAMMITE WOMAN'S STORY

THIS POETRY WAS PROBABLY WRITTEN AROUND 970–930 BC.

The Song of Songs is a spicy book—a set of romantic dialogue between a woman and her lover. It is also chock-full of literal mentions of spices and aromatics: myrrh, frankincense, nard, saffron, calamus, cinnamon, aloe, and henna. Together, these symbolized a life of abundance, and they were highly prized for their healing properties and their ability to flavor food. They were also used to adorn brides and were key ingredients in perfume and holy oils. Additionally, they were linked to the rich garden imagery that weaves its way through the poem.

Though the book is attributed to Solomon, he probably did not write it. Instead, it's more likely that the Song of Songs grew out of the wisdom tradition of Solomon. But what are love poems even doing in the Bible? Scholars have been asking that question for centuries. Many modern commentators view Song of Songs simply as an example of love poetry common to the Ancient Near East.

Throughout their history, Jews have understood it as something more—not merely as a romantic text but as a beautiful representation of the love between Yahweh and Israel, with God as the Bridegroom and Israel as his bride. Christians have thought of it as a book depicting the love between Christ and the church (Ephesians 5:25-33) or Christ and the individual soul.

However you understand the Song, you cannot ignore its sensuality. In the opening scene, the Shulammite woman takes the initiative. In most Ancient Near Eastern literature men take the lead in romantic relationships while women are pictured in idealized and passive roles. But this woman speaks boldly and more frequently than her male counterpart, something that would have astonished anyone who read or listened to these poems in the time they were written.

Let him kiss me with the kisses of his
mouth—

for your love is more delightful than
wine . . . .
No wonder the young women love you!
Take me away with you—let us hurry!
Let the king bring me into his chambers (Song of Songs 1:2-4).

Notice that the Shulammite woman doesn't meet her lover in a chronological sequence. Rather than following a linear narrative, Song of Songs cycles between voices and also between themes of love, longing, and beauty. Because of this and because ancient Judaism did not condone premarital sex, it would be a mistake to read it as though it is approving of sexual intimacy outside of marriage.

What about all the lush garden imagery and the profusion of spices mentioned in the book? Think back to Genesis 1-2 where Adam and Eve lived together in a beautiful garden filled with every kind of plant. The lovers in Song of Songs help us to imagine what their relationship may have been like had they obeyed God and continued to live in Eden.

In the beginning, harmony, mutual desire, and equality existed between male and female. But after the fall, a note of dominance appears (Genesis 3:16). In the Song, the lovers speak as equals (Song of Songs 6:3) and have no shame about their desires. In Genesis, Adam and Eve's original innocence (Genesis 2:25) gave way to an attempt to hide their nakedness (Genesis 3:6-7). For these and other reasons, some commentators view the imagery in the Song as purposely depicting an Eden-like relationship. We can learn something from all these interpretations—another reason this book is celebrated as the song of all songs.

THE SHULAMMITE WOMAN'S *Legacy* IN SCRIPTURE

READ

Song of Songs 4:9-5:1

- Explain how this love poem supports or opposes how you view:

  Romantic love

  Married love

- What part does physical beauty play in Song of Songs, and how important is it in a love relationship?

- What picture of married love do you get from these verses?

- What is your response when you look at this as a picture of God's love for you?

READ

Song of Songs 8:6-7

- What symbols do these verses use to illustrate love? What part of love does each of them represent?

- Compare the way love is portrayed in these verses to how our culture today views and depicts love.

- What does it take to sustain the committed love experienced by the Shulammite woman?

OUR *Connection* TO THE SHULAMMITE WOMAN

Who is this passionate woman who can't wait to be united to her lover? The word *Shulammite* may indicate that she was from the town of Shulem, in northern Israel, or it may be, as some suggest, that her name is a feminine form of the name Solomon. She describes herself as being dark-skinned from working outdoors (Song of Songs 1:6), which may mean she has a rural and humble background. Speaking first, she is bold in her longing and ardent in her love.

- How does the Song of Songs resonate with your own experience of love, longing, and spiritual searching?

- How do the words and images align or not align with your views about how Jesus wants to relate to you?

- Is it possible that desire, in addition to obedience, can become a pathway to God? Why or why not?

"Jesus, lover of my soul, let me to thy bosom fly."[11] Burn your love so deep within me that I have no response except to love you as I have been loved. Thank you, Savior, for a love so deep that you willingly gave your life for mine.

11 Charles Wesley, "Jesus Lover of My Soul," 1740.

WEEK 35

GOMER

HER NAME MAY MEAN "COMPLETION" OR "FINISHED."

Her Story

The unfaithful wife of the prophet Hosea, Gomer's story symbolized God's continued love for his unfaithful people.

"I will heal their waywardness and love them freely, for my anger has turned away from them." HOSEA 14:4

READ

Hosea 1-3

Who WAS SHE?

God ordered the prophet Hosea to marry a promiscuous woman, one guaranteed to be unfaithful to him. Hosea obeyed the difficult command, marrying Gomer. Together they had three children, each of which was given an unfortunate name related to Israel's unfaithfulness. These names served as living prophecies of impending judgment. When Hosea later redeemed his promiscuous wife, the renaming of their children became a powerful symbol of God's enduring compassion and mercy toward his people after their punishment.

A *Closer Look* AT GOMER'S STORY

HER STORY TOOK PLACE AROUND 750–722 BC.

Wouldn't it be great to have God write your love story?

Not if your name was Hosea, a prophet who lived in Israel. His "match made in heaven" was with a woman named Gomer, an Israelite who fit the description God provided—"a promiscuous woman" or, literally, "a wife of whoredom" (Hosea 1:2 ESV). But who would wish for such a wife?

Their story took place during a period when widespread prosperity in the Northern Kingdom was giving way to growing political instability. Over a period of twenty-five years, six kings had ruled. Their successors murdered four to gain the throne, and one perished in battle. To the north, the great Assyrian power gathered steam like an active volcano ready to hurl out its armies. Pity anyone in its path.

Israel's position was precarious. Elijah and Elisha had resisted the spiritual unfaithfulness of God's people by warning of judgment. But Israel kept backsliding. In addition to trampling the poor, they sacrificed at pagan high places, visited sacred prostitutes, and worshiped idols. No matter how dire the warnings or how spectacular the miracles, stubborn, wanton Israel refused to listen. Then God decided to try something new. He would reveal his heart through flesh and blood. He would do it by uniting two ill-matched people—Hosea and Gomer—in holy matrimony.

In the course of time, Gomer gave birth to three children. God told Hosea to name the first boy Jezreel, meaning "God scatters." He named the second, a girl, Lo-Ruhamah, meaning "not loved." The third, another boy, he named Lo-Ammi, meaning "not my people." Hosea wondered if the last two were even his. After that Gomer abandoned her husband and children to pursue other loves.

Instead of divorcing her, Hosea pursued her, following the Lord's admonition to "Go, show your love to your wife again, though she is loved by another man and is an adulteress. Love her as the LORD loves the Israelites" (Hosea 3:1). By the time Hosea tracked her down, Gomer had sunk into a pit of debt so deep she couldn't climb out. Instead of abandoning her, Hosea spent everything he had to pay off her debt, then reclaimed her as his own.

What a stunning portrait of love! Not just of one human being toward another but of God toward his people, of God loving us! Later in the book, Hosea diagnosed Israel's condition, saying that the people had become as "vile as the thing they loved" (Hosea 9:10). Turning away from God had disfigured and blinded them. They could no longer look in the mirror and recognize themselves as God's beloved. Even so, God still loved them and refused to divorce them.

As Gomer's story draws to a close, Jezreel becomes "God plants" rather than "God scatters," Lo-Ruhamah transforms into "the one God loves," and Lo-Ammi becomes "God's people." Upon returning home, Gomer—and Israel—find out who they really are, but only in the arms of their true husband.

GOMER'S *Legacy* IN SCRIPTURE

READ

Hosea 1:2–2:7; 3

- What kind of a man was Hosea? What kind of a woman was Gomer? How does their relationship parallel God's relationship with Israel?

- How do you respond to the names and their meaning for each of Gomer's children?

READ

Hosea 3

- God speaks of love in all his directives to Hosea regarding Gomer. What does this tell you about God's love for you?

- Picture yourself as Hosea. What are you thinking?

- Picture yourself as Gomer. What are you feeling?

- Explore the ways God has pursued you as Hosea pursued Gomer.

OUR *Connection* TO GOMER

Despite the cautionary love story of Hosea and Gomer, Israel fell to Assyria in 722 BC. Though Hosea prophesied prior to the exile, the final compilation of the book of Hosea may have taken place in the Southern Kingdom of Judah after the Assyrian invasion in the north. Its twin notes of love and repentance would have generated both warning and hope in those who read it.

> "Come, let us return to the LORD.
> He has torn us to pieces
>   but he will heal us;
> he has injured us
>   but he will bind up our wounds . . . .
> Let us acknowledge the LORD;
>   let us press on to acknowledge him.

As surely as the sun rises,
he will appear;
he will come to us like the winter rains,
like the spring rains that water the earth" (Hosea 6:1, 3).

When Gomer's story begins, the Israelites are like everyone around them. What similarities do you see between her culture and ours?

How might your understanding of repentance change if you were to think of it in terms of coming home to the God who loves you?

Dear Father, what a difficult time I have admitting that I, too, am prone to wandering. Bring me back to yourself so that I can recognize who you are, and thereby know who I am . . . your beloved child.

WEEK 36

ELIZABETH

"GOD IS MY OATH"

Her Story

The God of the impossible stepped in when Elizabeth was far beyond childbearing years, enabling her to become the mother of John the Baptist, the forerunner of Jesus.

"Elizabeth your relative is going to have a child in her old age, and she who was said to be unable to conceive is in her sixth month." LUKE 1:36

READ

Luke 1:5-80

Who WAS SHE?

Elizabeth joined the long line of Israelite women whom God miraculously enabled to conceive when pregnancy seemed impossible. An angel announced to her priestly husband that they would have a son despite their old age—a message he struggled to believe. That son would grow up to proclaim the arrival of the Messiah. In a remarkable confirmation of God's promise, when Elizabeth encountered the young woman carrying the Messiah, the child within her "leaped for joy" (Luke 1:44).

A *Closer Look* AT ELIZABETH'S STORY

HER STORY TOOK PLACE AROUND 7–4 BC.

A long thread wove its way through the Old Testament and straight into the New. It stitched together the stories of Sarah, Rebekah, Rachel, Hannah, and now Elizabeth. Soon it would make its way into Mary's story too. Each woman had her own joyful tale of an impossible pregnancy, a story of God keeping his promises. But then nothing is impossible for God (Luke 1:37).

Elizabeth and her husband, Zechariah, were like restyled versions of Abraham and Sarah, too old for children but pregnant nonetheless. Zechariah was a doubter like Sarah. While she smothered her laughter when she heard an angel promise motherhood (Genesis 18:10-15), Zechariah interrogated the angel to his face, saying, "How can I be sure of this? I am an old man and my wife is well along in years" (Luke 1:18). For his refusal to believe in the answer to his own prayer, despite it being delivered by an angel, and for his inability to remember what God had done for Sarah, the angel censured him, saying he would not be able to speak until his son was born.

But Elizabeth grabbed hold of the promise right away, proclaiming, "The Lord has done this for me. . . . In these days he has shown his favor and taken away my disgrace among the people" (Luke 1:25).

Elizabeth would have known about disgrace, the shaming that came when there was no child, especially a son to carry on her husband's name. Then God appeared, erasing her dishonor, gifting her with a child—and not just any child. This one would become a spectacular man. John the Baptist would "go on before the Lord, in the spirit and power of Elijah, to turn the hearts of the parents to their children and the disobedient to the wisdom of the righteous—to make ready a people prepared for the Lord" (Luke 1:17).

Both Elizabeth and Zechariah belonged to the tribe of Levi. As one of Israel's ten thousand priests in first-century Israel, Zechariah had been chosen by lot to keep incense burning in front of the Most Holy Place, a once-in-a-lifetime opportunity. The incense symbolized the prayers of God's people ascending to the throne of

God. In answer to those prayers, which had been piling up for centuries, an angel appeared to Zechariah. Significantly, the angel stood at the right side of the altar—a position that symbolized honor, favor, and the presence of God.

Six months later, Zechariah's pregnant wife and unborn child would become the first to recognize Mary's unborn baby as the long-promised Messiah. The moment Elizabeth heard Mary's greeting, her child leaped in her womb. Filled with the Holy Spirit, she shouted, "Blessed are you among women, and blessed is the child you will bear! . . . Blessed is she who has believed that the Lord would fulfill his promises to her!" (Luke 1:42, 45).

How Elizabeth's faith must have comforted Mary, the unmarried teenager, who was bearing the Savior of the world!

ELIZABETH'S *Legacy* IN SCRIPTURE

READ

Luke 1:5-10

- Casting lots to discern God's will was common in the Old Testament (Leviticus 16:8; Joshua 18:8-10) and even in the New Testament (Acts 1:26). Why do you think the New Testament never mentions the practice again after Pentecost, when the Holy Spirit descended on believers (Acts 2)?

- God waited until bearing a child was physically impossible before he fulfilled Elizabeth's desire. How have you had to wait forever for God to fulfill your desires? How might Elizabeth's faithfulness and patience inspire you?

READ

Luke 1:11-20, 41-45

- Contrast Zechariah losing his voice with Elizabeth praising God with hers. Explore the reasons for this.

- Have you ever been moved to praise God like Elizabeth did? If so, when? If not, what sort of event might it take for you to respond as Elizabeth did?

- What does it tell you that Elizabeth praised God for what he was doing in young Mary's life rather than her own?

OUR *Connection* TO ELIZABETH

The Bible described Elizabeth and Zechariah as faithful Jews. Instead of letting her disappointment at being childless twist her into a bitter, angry, and hopeless old woman, Elizabeth exhibited great faith and a strong sensitivity to the Holy Spirit. Though often characterized as Mary's cousin, Scripture simply describes her as a relative. She may have been Mary's aunt. How beautifully Luke's Gospel weaves the story of these two women together, with the older encouraging and affirming the younger at a time of great vulnerability.

- Reread Luke 1:5-80, noting passages that mention joy or rejoicing in response to God's promises. How have you experienced this joy in your own life?

- Who has encouraged you, and who are you encouraging?

- Though Zechariah first responded with doubt to the angel's message, after the birth of his son he responded prophetically. How can his song (Luke 1:67-79) inspire you to live with faith and without fear?

God of the impossible and of promises fulfilled, we need you today. In a world characterized by hopelessness and broken promises, help us to remember you. Fill us with faith in you and you alone. Give us courage to live conspicuously as people who belong to you.

WEEK 37

MARY

THE MOTHER OF JESUS

HER NAME MAY MEAN "BITTERNESS" OR "BELOVED."

Her Story

God promised the betrothed but not-yet-wed Mary that she would have a son. He would be the long-promised Messiah, and she believed and accepted every word.

"I am the Lord's servant," Mary answered. "May your word to me be fulfilled." LUKE 1:38

READ

Matthew 1:18-2:23; Luke 1:26-56; John 19:25-27

Who WAS SHE?

Mary reacted with understandable fear when an angel appeared with the astonishing news that she would bear a son who would inherit the throne of the great King David. Unmarried and a virgin, she asked the angel in the frankest way possible how this could be. He responded mysteriously, saying that the Holy Spirit would "overshadow" her, and the child would be "holy" (Luke 1:35). As overwhelming as this must have felt, Mary responded with an unequivocal yes, an act of pure faith that has resounded across the centuries.

A *Closer Look* AT MARY, THE MOTHER OF JESUS' STORY

HER STORY TOOK PLACE AROUND 7 BC–AD 33.

Matthew's Gospel opens with a surprising account of Jesus' family tree. Surprising because his genealogy is not limited to males, as was usual, but includes five females. What's more, the mention of these women—Tamar, Rahab, Ruth, Uriah's wife (Bathsheba), and Mary, the teenage mother of Jesus—would hardly have boosted Jesus' status. How could it when two of these women were Gentiles and four were under suspicion of committing sexual immorality? Matthew, it seems, began his account of the good news by "reverse boasting" about the ancestry of Jesus.

Already, subtly, the gospel emerges as something surprising and disruptive. It turns the usual way of doing business upside down. That pattern continues with the story of a young woman named Mary and her fiancé, Joseph, who lived in the backwater town of Nazareth, a village of less than five hundred people. She was a nobody on the world stage, or even on Israel's small stage, but God favored her in an extraordinary way. Because of Mary's yes to his invitation, the unsettling upheaval of the gospel gathered steam.

We hear it already in her great song, later named the Magnificat, with its loud echoes of Hannah's song (1 Samuel 2:1–10). After the pregnant Elizabeth greeted her and called her blessed (Luke 1:45), Mary made several extraordinary claims. Though she and everyone she knew was suffocating under Roman oppression, she envisioned reality not according to her own circumstances but according to God's promises, exclaiming,

> "He has brought down rulers from their
> thrones
> but has lifted up the humble.
> He has filled the hungry with good
> things
> but has sent the rich away empty"
> (Luke 1:52–53).

Given the trajectory of her life, how can we think of Mary as anyone other than a woman filled with faith, courage, and deep spiritual insight, which would only have increased as she pondered the life of her son? No wonder she has been hailed with such superlatives as Jesus' "first disciple," the "new Eve," and the "first Christian theologian"!

Mary's yes to the angel Gabriel didn't come cheap. She would have known that her unexplained pregnancy could subject her to shunning and violence, maybe even to death. That may be why Joseph took her with him to Bethlehem despite how difficult the journey would have been for a pregnant woman (Luke 2:1-5). He may have feared the treatment she would suffer back home in his absence.[12]

When she and her small family visited the temple, Simeon's prophecy foretold future pain: "A sword will pierce your own soul too" (Luke 2:34-35). Mary could have chosen an easier path. But then she wouldn't have been the blessed woman Elizabeth had greeted. A woman who helped usher in Jesus' upside-down kingdom, a place where the poor and the lowly—the beatitude people (Matthew 5:3-10)—would displace the privileged and power-hungry as those who inherit the earth.

---

12 Bailey, Kenneth, "Women in the New Testament—Mary the Mother of Jesus," YouTube, September 21, 2020, 30:02.

MARY, THE MOTHER OF JESUS' *Legacy* IN SCRIPTURE

READ

Luke 1:26-38

Imagine yourself as a young teenager listening to the words of the angel Gabriel. What thoughts and feelings do you experience? How does this inform your understanding of what happened to Mary?

- In what life circumstances might you need to repeat Mary's words to God from Luke 1:38? Honestly assess what might make it hard or easy to say these words and truly mean them.

READ
Luke 1:39-45

- Why did Mary leave Nazareth to visit her relative Elizabeth?

- What might she have been hoping to find there? How might these events have encouraged or inspired Mary?

READ
Luke 2

- What does Luke 2:19, 51 tell you about how Mary processed early events in Jesus' life? What does this say about the kind of woman she was? Reflect on how being more like Mary could benefit you.

- What sort of "sword" did Simeon prophesy over Mary in Luke 2:35? What did this prophecy mean for Mary?

OUR *Connection* TO MARY, THE MOTHER OF JESUS

Blessed though she was, becoming the mother of Jesus put a spiritual target on Mary's back and endangered the life of her family. Herod the Great was a cruel puppet king, placed on the throne by Rome. A paranoiac who murdered his mother-in-law, wife, brother-in-law, and three of his own sons—he also massacred all the male infants of Bethlehem but one—because Jesus had already escaped with Mary and Joseph to Egypt. Their journey as refugees and their eventual return home recalled the exile of the Israelites to Egypt and their entry into the promised land (Matthew 2:13-23).

- How is Herod a new pharaoh and Jesus a new Moses in this particular story?

- Mary said yes to the full plan of God even though she didn't know what that fullness would entail. How are you being called to imitate her faith?

- What are the promises you need to continue to envision and believe even though they haven't yet been fulfilled?

Father, with Mary "my soul glorifies the Lord and my spirit rejoices in God my Savior" (Luke 1:46-47). You are watching over me just as you watched over Mary so long ago. Make me humble, like Mary, and thankful for your mercy and grace.

WEEK 38

ANNA

"FAVOR" OR "GRACE"

Her Story

As a prophet, the widow Anna was among the first to recognize Jesus as the long-promised Messiah.

A prophet, Anna . . . gave thanks to God and spoke about the child. LUKE 2:36, 38

READ

Luke 2:22-38

Who WAS SHE?

The atmosphere in the temple vibrated with anticipation. Mary and Joseph could have slipped in and out quietly when they went to perform the purification rites and present their son to the Lord. Yet the Holy Spirit had other plans. Stationed in the temple were two elderly prophets: Anna, one of only a handful of named female prophets in the Bible, and Simeon. Just as the law prescribed, God had provided two witnesses to testify that this was no ordinary child but the long-awaited Messiah (Deuteronomy 19:15; Matthew 18:16).

A *Closer Look* AT ANNA'S STORY

HER STORY TOOK PLACE AROUND 6–4 BC.

Six hundred years after the Babylonians destroyed Jerusalem and carried its people into exile, as Huldah had foretold (2 Kings 22:15-20), an elderly prophet named Anna was living in Jerusalem. Day after day for years on end, she spent all her time in the rebuilt temple, fasting and praying. During her life she would have witnessed thousands of people going in and out of the temple. How is it that on one particular day, she recognized one particular child who would change the history of her people and, indeed, the history of the world?

Forty days after his birth, Mary and Joseph brought their baby to the temple for the purification rites prescribed by the law of Moses (Leviticus 12). After giving birth, the law required women to offer a sacrifice for purification. Ritual purity wasn't about moral failure or sin, but about one's ceremonial fitness to enter sacred spaces like the temple. Since the Israelites worshiped God as the source of life, they believed that anyone who came into contact with something that might result in the loss of life (things like childbirth, illnesses, skin diseases, or bodily fluids) would become ritually impure.

In addition to performing the purification rites, Mary and Joseph brought Jesus to the temple to consecrate him to God. This practice linked back to the exodus when God spared the firstborn sons of the Israelite slaves in the tenth plague. By dedicating their firstborn sons, with their special status and privileged rights of inheritance, they were acknowledging that God alone was the source of every blessing and the ultimate authority, regardless of how society organized itself.

Anna would have seen countless ordinary couples enter the temple to perform the same rites that Jesus' parents were performing. But because of her prophetic gifting and unusual spiritual sensitivity, she came upon the small family at the precise moment the prophet Simeon was praising God, saying:

> "Sovereign Lord, as you have promised,
> you may now dismiss your servant in peace.
> For my eyes have seen your salvation,

which you have prepared in the
sight of all nations:
a light for revelation to the Gentiles,
and the glory of your people Israel"
(Luke 2:29–32).

By including two prophets in this poignant scene, the Bible telegraphed that Jesus' mission was closely connected to the temple, the place twelve-year-old Jesus would later call "my Father's house" (Luke 2:49). By including both sexes, it also pointed to the fact that the good news would include everyone. No one would be left out of the invitation to participate in the inbreaking kingdom of God. While Simeon was content to be "dismissed in peace," eighty-four-year-old Anna couldn't stop speaking about Jesus.

Anna's *Legacy* in Scripture

READ

Luke 2:22–38

- Look closely at verses 32 and 38. What do these prophecies from Simeon and Anna tell you about Jesus' mission?

- Why were people at that time longing and praying for the Messiah to come? What does that tell you about how they thought and how they might have lived their lives? Consider in your answers the situation in Israel at that time, where they were suffering under a cruel Roman government.

- Describe the sort of life Anna led at this time. What aspects of it seem attractive or foreign to you?

- What do you long to see God accomplish before you die?

OUR *Connection* TO ANNA

How did Anna manage to stay in the temple day and night, fasting and praying? Though the women's court had no private rooms, it did have covered areas that could allow for prolonged stays. However, "never left" (Luke 2:37) may not have meant she stayed there 24/7 but that she completely centered her life in the temple. What is most obvious about Anna is that she was a woman consumed by a desire to do God's will, so devout that she spent every ounce of her energy seeking the God she loved.

- How might Anna's total devotion challenge your assumptions about the most productive way to use your time?

- Widows were often the most vulnerable people in ancient Israel. Elderly widows even more so. Yet Anna was spiritually vigorous. How might her story challenge our society's views about age, gender, and ministry effectiveness? Whom do you know—male or female—who exemplifies her virtues?

Father, help me to be inspired rather than intimidated by Anna's example. Give me a spirit like hers, a dedication and love for you that drives and fulfills me and enables me to serve you passionately.

WEEK 39

THE WOMAN OF SAMARIA

Her Story

God chose an outsider and a sinner to spread the good news of the Messiah to her people.

Many of the Samaritans from that town believed in him because of the woman's testimony. JOHN 4:39

READ
John 4:1-42

Who WAS SHE?

The Samaritan woman—marginalized by both her people's history and her own reputation—was the first person to whom Jesus plainly revealed his identity as the Messiah without parable or cloaked language. Transformed by this encounter, she became the first evangelist, hurrying to her village to proclaim that the Messiah had come. Drawn by her testimony, the townspeople returned to the well and met Jesus for themselves. Many came to believe in him as "the Savior of the world" (John 4:42).

A *Closer Look* AT THE WOMAN OF SAMARIA'S STORY

HER STORY TOOK PLACE AROUND AD 26–30.

When Assyria defeated the Northern Kingdom of Israel in 722 BC, it exiled part of the population and imported foreigners to take their place. This brutal policy served to weaken national identity and prevent insurgencies.

The Samaritans emerged as a group formed by intermarriage between the new immigrants and the remaining Israelites. The Jews of Jesus' day considered Samaritans half-breeds, apostates, and idolaters. That's why it's surprising that Jesus and his disciples decided to cut through Samaria on their way to Galilee. Most Jews took the longer route to avoid contact with the despised Samaritans.

Sending his disciples to the nearest town for provisions, Jesus met a woman alone at a well, and not just any well. This was the patriarch Jacob's well, dug at least seventeen hundred years earlier.

Meetings at wells in the Bible are often associated with courtship, betrothal, and marriage. Abraham's servant met Rebekah at a well in his quest to find a wife for Isaac (Genesis 24:10-27), Jacob met Rachel at a well (Genesis 29:1-12), and Moses met his future wife, Zipporah, at a well (Exodus 2:15-22).

But the woman at this well was hardly a good marriage prospect, not with her history of five husbands and the fact that she was not married to the man with whom she was now living. When Jesus revealed that he knew these things about her, something shifted.

Though Jacob's well was old and deep, recalling the covenant God made with his people because of its association with the patriarch, Jesus spoke about something new and even deeper—living water welling up to eternal life. He also spoke about something much broader. No longer would true worship be confined to one geographic location, Jerusalem. Instead, the worship the Father desired would break out everywhere.

Instead of a temple that would restrict Gentiles, including Samaritans, to the outermost courtyard and women to the women's courtyard, these boundaries would vanish. Everyone, regardless of their status, would be invited to draw near to the Father to worship him in spirit and in truth.

When the woman of Samaria responded by saying that the Messiah would explain everything when he came, Jesus replied with the astonishing words "I am he" (John 4:26). Then she ran back to town, leaving her water jar behind, saying to anyone who would listen, "Come, see a man who told me everything I ever did" (verse 29). As a result, many of the Samaritans became believers.

Perhaps Jesus' meeting with the woman at Jacob's well forged not only a symbolic bridge between the old and new covenants but served as a betrothal story after all. For, like a lover who will let nothing separate him from his beloved, Jesus crossed every boundary—ethnic, moral, religious, and gender—in order to reach out to this woman and her fellow Samaritans. Even when he revealed her marital situation, it was to bring it into the open so she could be reconciled to him. If that's not a beautiful love story, what is?

THE WOMAN OF SAMARIA'S *Legacy* IN SCRIPTURE

READ

John 4:4-42

- Trace the Samaritan woman's emotional responses as her encounter with Jesus unfolds. Describe what she may have been feeling in verses 7-9, 10-12, 13-15, 16, 17-20, and 21-26.

- Looking at her life, what do you think this woman was thirsty for?

- What have you used to try to satisfy your spiritual thirst apart from Christ? Family? Career? Money? Entertainment? Something else?

- What does Jesus mean by worshiping "in the Spirit and in truth" (John 4:23-24)?

- Why do you think Jesus chose to reveal his true identity for the first time to this woman, an outcast of society, instead of to the leaders of the Jewish religion or even to his own disciples?

- If Jesus truly is the Savior who knows everything you ever did, what can the Samaritan woman teach you about how to respond to him today?

OUR *Connection* TO THE WOMAN OF SAMARIA

This woman may not have been as immoral as some have painted her. Widowhood, abandonment, or divorce would have left her economically dependent, perhaps impoverished, without anyone to support her. Nevertheless, her appearance at the well in the middle of the day, when the sun was at its hottest, rather than in the morning or early evening when other women gathered, suggests she was a social outcast. Whatever caused her situation, two things are true: She was the first person to whom Jesus openly identified himself as the Messiah, and she was also the first person to spread the good news.

- The Samaritan woman went to the well to get water. At the end of her story, she left her water jar behind. What do you make of this detail?

- Imagine yourself as the woman at the well. As Jesus speaks to you, what are you thinking? How do you respond?

Jesus, my Savior, just like the Samaritan woman, I carry my own past and brokenness. As I seek you and as you reveal yourself to me, make me more like her—bold and joyful, eager to share with others the good news of how you have saved me and have come to save the world!

WEEK 40

THE SINFUL WOMAN

Her Story

In a public and dramatic act of thanksgiving, she washed Jesus' feet with her tears and anointed them with costly perfume. He lifted her up, declaring her forgiven and at peace.

"I tell you, her many sins have been forgiven—as her great love has shown." LUKE 7:47

READ
Luke 7:36-50

Who WAS SHE?

She slipped quietly along the wall behind the Pharisee's guests, searching for one person—the healer, the teacher, the one capable of restoring her shattered life. Kneeling at Jesus' feet, her tears fell freely, washing the dust from his feet as she used her unbound hair to gently dry them. Then, with trembling hands, she poured out precious perfume in an act of love and devotion. The murmurs around her faded until only his words filled her heart: "Your sins are forgiven" (Luke 7:48). Because of him she was no longer the sinful woman but the forgiven woman.

A *Closer Look* AT THE SINFUL WOMAN'S STORY

HER STORY TOOK PLACE AROUND AD 26–30.

This story is distinct from others in the Gospels of Matthew, Mark, and John where a woman anointed Jesus. Probably a prostitute, this woman must have welcomed the gospel Jesus preached as the best news she had ever heard.[13] But how did she end up in a Pharisee's house?

Opening your home to the needy when you were hosting a meal was a custom that showcased your generosity. But the woman in this story may not have been poor, only determined. She wanted one thing: to express her gratitude to the man who had taught her about God's incredible love for sinners.

From the moment Jesus entered the home, she would have noticed Simon's rudeness as he publicly humiliated the young rabbi by withholding the customary kiss on the cheek and the water and olive oil for washing and anointing himself.

The dining area may have been organized as a *triclinium*, whereby three couches were arranged in a rectangular pattern, leaving the fourth side open for servants to come and go with food and drink. A guest would recline on his left side, prop himself up on his left elbow, and use his right hand to procure food from a tray or low table.

In this case, those waiting patiently for leftovers would have sat against the wall while the woman would have knelt at the back of the couch, where Jesus' feet were visible. Simon had provided no water for Jesus' feet, so she would provide her tears. He had provided no towel to wipe them, so she would provide her hair. Then she kissed his feet and anointed them with expensive perfume. Uncovering her hair in public would have been considered indecent, an act that could subject a married woman to divorce.

Though Simon was incensed by her outrageous behavior, Jesus praised her

13 For a fascinating interpretation of this woman's story, upon which much of this piece is drawn, see Kenneth E. Bailey, *Jesus Through Middle Eastern Eyes* (Intervarsity Press, 2008), 239–260.

actions because they revealed her total devotion to him, showcasing how deeply she felt his humiliation. He must also have known that criticism from him would have shattered her.

Instead of being offended by her behavior, Jesus turned to Simon and asked a series of provocative questions. Would Simon continue to focus his attention on the perceived sins of others, or would he look inside and see his own failures? Would he double down on his own righteousness, or would he follow this woman's beautiful example and receive the forgiveness that Jesus graciously offered? Though we may be tempted to focus on Simon's shortcomings, these are questions that are also meant for us. In essence, the question to be answered is this: Do we want to love much or love little?

THE SINFUL WOMAN'S *Legacy* IN SCRIPTURE

READ

Luke 7:36-50

- What did it cost this woman to do what she did?

- Could you be this open in expressing your love for Jesus? Why or why not?

- What would happen if a sexually promiscuous person or a drug addict or someone guilty of theft came to your Bible study and expressed their sin and need of forgiveness?

- How could you be more loving and accepting of those whose lives have been shattered by sin, like this woman? Or those whose lives are characterized by judgment, like the Pharisee? Who needs forgiveness more?

- Think deeply and honestly about your own sin and your own need for Jesus' forgiveness. Have you been forgiven much or little? Do you love much or little?

OUR *Connection* TO THE SINFUL WOMAN

People wore sandals as they walked along roads littered with refuse and debris. If it rained, the dust would turn into a muddy mixture of dirt and animal waste. That's why foot washing was not a luxury but a necessity, and why it was performed by the lowest household servant or slave. The woman in this story used her body—her tears, her hair, her lips—to display her total devotion to Jesus.

- There are two kinds of sinners in this story—a law breaker and a law keeper. In what ways might law-keeping make it difficult for you to receive God's forgiveness?

- The sinful woman spent lavishly on Jesus, crossing social boundaries, risking censure, and pouring expensive perfume all over his feet. How might God be calling you to spend lavishly on Jesus right now?

Jesus, I admit I often resemble the judgmental Pharisee more than the needy and sinful woman. Help me to recognize the depth of my sin and need for your forgiveness. I kneel before you and pour out my heart at your feet.

WEEK 41

THE WOMAN WITH THE ISSUE OF BLOOD

Her Story

Depleted by chronic bleeding and depressed by her isolation, this woman reached out her hand toward the healer, her last hope.

Jesus turned and saw her. "Take heart, daughter," he said, "your faith has healed you." And the woman was healed at that moment. MATTHEW 9:22

READ

Matthew 9:20-22; Mark 5:25-34; Luke 8:43-48

Who WAS SHE?

After twelve years of relentless bleeding, her body weakened, her resources spent on false healers, and her spirit crushed by rejection, this woman was nearing the brink of despair. She believed that Jesus could heal her—but would he, without knowing her or being touched by her? Fearful of defiling him, she took a daring step. Weaving through the crowd, she reached out and lightly touched the edge of his cloak. In an instant, she felt it—complete, miraculous restoration. She was healed, fully and utterly, as life and hope flooded back into her body.

A *Closer Look* AT THE WOMAN WITH THE ISSUE OF BLOOD'S STORY

HER STORY TOOK PLACE AROUND AD 26–30.

The story of this woman, suffering for twelve years with what was probably a uterine hemorrhage, touches us. Picture someone with extreme fatigue and weakness, dizziness, sallow skin, and possibly heart palpitations. She may have experienced pelvic pain and infertility, growing thin as her muscles wasted away. Without successful treatment, her condition would worsen until it threatened her life.

It also would have cut her off from the life of the community, not because of moral failure, but because her disorder made her ritually impure. Unable to participate in worship, she would have transmitted her uncleanness to anyone she touched. It would not be surprising if her prolonged isolation provoked bouts of loneliness, depression, and shame.

By the time she met Jesus, after having spent her last cent on a cure, she was desperate. A crushing crowd surrounded him when a synagogue leader fell to his knees before Jesus, begging him to save his daughter who was deathly ill. The woman quietly approached from behind, reaching out to touch the edge of his garment. The Greek word in Matthew 9:20 is *kraspedon*, which can be translated "edge," "border," or "fringe" of a garment. In this case it refers to cloth tassels (*tzitzit*) interwoven with blue thread, attached to the four corners of Jesus' outer cloak, as commanded by Numbers 15:37–41. These tassels acted as a reminder of God's commandments.

According to later rabbinic tradition, the tassels symbolized heaven and earth being woven together, with the tassels representing earth and the blue thread representing the sapphire sea, the sky, and the throne of God in heaven. Imagine someone in ancient Israel kicking up dust as he walked along the road. As the dust of the earth stuck to the tassels, the blue thread shone in the sunlight with its reminder of heaven.

More than obeying the command to wear the tassels on his garment, Jesus perfectly embodied its symbolism. As he told his disciples after his encounter with the woman at the well, "My food . . . is to do the will of him who sent me and to finish his work" (John 4:34). It is not a stretch to imagine that when the bleeding woman touched the tassels attached to his garment, she touched the place where heaven and earth perfectly intersected in the person of Jesus. At that moment, power traveled from him to her. Instead of infecting him with her impurity, his purity healed her. His holiness, as some New Testament scholars have pointed out, is contagious in the opposite direction.

But the hem itself was not magic. Her faith combined with Jesus' power effected the miracle. When Jesus called her "daughter" and commended her for her faith (Mark 5:34), he not only healed her body but affirmed her identity, restoring her dignity so she could take her place at the center of God's family.

THE WOMAN WITH THE ISSUE OF BLOOD'S *Legacy* IN SCRIPTURE

READ

Mark 5:24-34

- Choose three words to describe the kinds of suffering this woman had been experiencing for twelve years.

- Why was this woman considered unclean (see Leviticus 15:19-31)? She likely accidentally touched a number of people in the crowd before getting to Jesus. What was she risking by doing this? What did it take to accept such a risk?

- Describe what this woman might have felt in the moment she was healed.

- Why do you think she was afraid to admit she was the one who had touched Jesus' cloak?

- If you have asked Jesus for healing and haven't yet received it, what do you do with this story?

OUR *Connection* TO THE WOMAN WITH THE ISSUE OF BLOOD

Though the crowd pressed against him, Jesus seemed to have felt the touch of only one person—a woman who boldly disregarded laws that would have prevented her from coming to him. She put her faith into action, and that is what touched him. Her story points to Jesus as the new and greater Temple, whereby the presence of God moved into the person of Christ. It also hints at something yet to come. To be in contact with a dead person or even a dead animal would have rendered a person ritually unclean. But Jesus' death on a cross did not defile him. Instead, his power worked in the opposite direction, swallowing up death so that we could have life.

- What does the woman's trembling response to Jesus in Luke 8:47 reveal about the tension between fear and faith?

- How have you put your own faith into action? Be as specific as possible.

- How have you experienced the healing power of Jesus in your life, physically, spiritually, socially, and emotionally?

Jesus, increase my faith and diminish my fear. When healing comes, I'll praise you. And if it doesn't, I will continue to trust you.

WEEK 42

HERODIAS

HER NAME IS THE FEMALE FORM OF HEROD AND MEANS "HEROIC."

Her Story

A princess in Herod's household, she despised John the Baptist and was responsible for his death.

Herod himself had given orders to have John arrested, and he had him bound and put in prison. He did this because of Herodias. MARK 6:17

READ

Matthew 14:3-12; Mark 6:14-29

Who WAS SHE?

Herodias grew up as part of the powerful family of Herod the Great, accustomed to privilege and influence. She did whatever she wished to satisfy her own desires without considering the consequences, perhaps feeling herself above them. When she grew bored with her first husband, she left him to marry his half brother, earning the outspoken criticism of John the Baptist. His public pronouncements so angered her that in time she connived John's execution.

A *Closer Look* AT HERODIAS'S STORY

HER STORY TOOK PLACE AROUND 27–29 BC.

Herodias was the granddaughter of Herod the Great, the paranoiac king who tried to kill the infant Jesus. His bloody legacy extended even to members of his own family, including Herodias's father, grandmother, and several of her uncles (Herod's sons). Her family was notorious for marital scandals, intrigues, and political murders.

To concentrate power within the royal family, she was wed to her uncle Herod Philip, a son of Herod the Great. According to the Jewish historian Josephus, she bore Philip a daughter named Salome. But when she tired of the marriage, she discarded Philip to wed another uncle, his half brother Herod Antipas, who, along with Pontius Pilate, would later preside over Jesus' trial in Jerusalem.

Though marrying your husband's brother while the former was still alive was against the Mosaic law, Herodias must have thought her privileged position would shield her from criticism. But a loud, persistent prophet by the name of John the Baptist, Elizabeth and Zechariah's son, wouldn't let the matter go. Clad in camel skin and a leather belt, subsisting on locusts and honey, he must have seemed like a rustic, wild man. Yet John was a new Elijah (Matthew 11:14), the fiery prophet who had challenged Jezebel and Ahab (1 Kings 17-19). Like him, John was not a man to weave and bob when it came to confronting corrupt political powers. Regardless of risk, he publicly rebuked Herod Antipas for marrying his brother's wife. Ever after, Herodias held a grudge so strong that it eventually led to murder.

To shut John up, Herod imprisoned him in Machaerus, a palatial stone fortress east of the Dead Sea. Perched on a mountaintop, deep ravines surrounded it on three sides, and it boasted a commanding view of the eastern frontier. Herod had mixed feelings about the popular prophet, thinking him a fascinating but dangerous man. Though he may have wanted to rid himself of John, he feared doing so lest his execution incite an insurrection.

John languished in prison until the day of Herod's fateful birthday party, in which Herodias's daughter, Salome, performed a seductive dance. For female family members to perform in front of a bunch of drunken men at a feast would have been shocking. But it served Herodias's purposes. She could not order John's execution, but she could leverage her husband's weakness. She knew that the rich food and flowing wine would go to his head. She also knew that he would not embarrass himself or risk his honor by rescinding a promise he had publicly made, no matter how rashly given.

If John was a new Elijah, Herodias was a new Jezebel, and Herod Antipas a new Ahab. Both prophets were bold. Both women were ruthless and manipulative, determined to get their way. Both kings were weak and subject to manipulation. Like their wives, they hardened their hearts when confronted with the truth. While John the Baptist feared God, Herod Antipas feared men, and Herodias feared no one.

HERODIAS'S *Legacy* IN SCRIPTURE

READ

Mark 6:14-29

- What in Herodias's background may have contributed to her wicked nature?

- What do the responses to John the Baptist in Mark 6:19-20, 26 tell you about Herod and about Herodias?

- When someone confronts you about a failing or sin, how are you likely to respond? Like Herodias? Like Herod? Or in some other way?

- Note the specific parts of this story that tell you Herodias was power-hungry and determined to get her way.

- What reaction do you have to Herodias's use of her daughter in her scheme?

- Have you ever been in a position when getting your way was exceptionally important to you? What did you do? What consequences did you face?

OUR *Connection* TO HERODIAS

Herod Antipas was governor of Galilee and Perea. As such, he held greater power than his half brother Herod Philip, which may be why Herodias left Philip to marry Antipas. Her ambition surfaced in AD 39 when the Roman Emperor Caligula named her brother Agrippa I king of a neighboring territory. She urged Herod Antipas to go to Rome to petition the emperor to make him a king as well. Her plans backfired when Agrippa I accused Herod of conspiracy and Caligula exiled him to Gaul. Though she could have stayed behind, Herodias chose to join her husband in exile. All their wealth and lands were forfeited to Agrippa.

- Because Herodias had little public authority, her influence operated behind the scenes. Have you ever been frustrated in a situation where you had no direct authority? How did you handle it? How did things turn out?

- When have you had the courage to confront power with truth as John did? Describe what happened. What did you learn?

Lord, power can be so corrupting. Please help me to recognize any tendency I may have to dominate others. Let a true heart of service, of goodness and kindness, grow in me instead.

WEEK 43

JOANNA

"YAHWEH IS GRACIOUS"

Her Story

Well-to-do and not afraid to challenge society's norms, Joanna traveled with Jesus and his disciples and supported them financially.

Joanna the wife of Chuza, the manager of Herod's household .... [helped] to support them out of their own means. LUKE 8:3

READ

Luke 8:1-3; 23:55-56; 24:1-2

Who WAS SHE?

According to Luke 8:2, Jesus had healed Joanna from an illness. Her gratitude turned into devotion expressed through practical generosity. Along with other women, she used her own resources to support Jesus and his disciples as they journeyed from place to place. Though they could have spent their wealth on personal comfort, they chose instead to give selflessly. Scripture honors them as women of courage and generosity—even when traveling alongside men defied the social expectations of their time.

A *Closer Look* AT JOANNA'S STORY

HER STORY TOOK PLACE AROUND AD 27–30.

As the wife of Chuza, the manager of Herod's household, Joanna would have belonged to an elite circle of high-status people in Herod's court. Participating in banquets, religious gatherings, and other social events meant that she probably knew both Herod Antipas and his wife Herodias.

She also knew Jesus, who early in his public ministry healed her of an illness. From the very beginning Jesus drew followers from every social stratum, even from the privileged social group to which Joanna belonged.

Luke's Gospel names Joanna, along with Mary Magdalene and Susanna, as one of the women who traveled with Jesus and his twelve disciples. These women provided practical and financial support for his itinerant ministry. Such a situation would have been astonishing, even scandalous, in first-century Israel, just as it would be in traditional Middle Eastern societies today.

Though wealthy women could be benefactors, a woman could never become the disciple of a rabbi unless the rabbi was her husband and he was willing to teach her.[14] Additionally, women didn't travel unless accompanied by a male guardian, usually a relative. One must put on first-century Jewish glasses to imagine just how scandalous Joanna's membership in Jesus' traveling entourage would have been.

The story of Joanna offers a glimpse of how Jesus persistently broke through social, cultural, and religious barriers between males and females as well as between the haves and the have-nots. The miracles he performed, the parables he told, and the way he responded to women all bore testimony to women's equal value. When Jesus healed the woman with the issue of blood, for instance (Mark 5:25-34),

14 Ben Witherington III, *Women and the Genesis of Christianity* (Cambridge University Press, 1990), 111.

he responded to her as someone who was neither defiled nor defiling. By healing her, he removed her unfitness, and, by implication, the unfitness of other women to participate in communal worship. No longer could ritual impurity prevent anyone from participating in the kingdom. Christ's attitude toward women enabled Joanna and many others to become full and important members of the Jesus community.[15]

Remarkably, Joanna was among the women who were the first to hear and bear testimony to the fact that Jesus, who had been tortured and crucified on a Roman cross, had risen from the dead.

15 Witherington III, *Women and the Genesis of Christianity*, 83–84.

JOANNA'S *Legacy* IN SCRIPTURE

READ

Luke 8:1-3

- What connection is there between Joanna's healing and her support of Jesus?

- Discuss what may have been unusual about Joanna and the other women traveling with Jesus. Where might they have gotten the financial means to do so?

- How does Joanna's generosity encourage the same in your own life?

- Describe the social barriers these women must have faced. What social barriers do women today face in ministry and discipleship?

READ

Luke 23:55-24:12

- How did the disciples react to the news from Joanna and the other women? Why do you think they responded this way?

- List some of Joanna's qualities that you would like to imitate.

OUR *Connection* TO JOANNA

Joanna followed Jesus for the entirety of his public ministry. While her social status would have bestowed wealth and influence, it may also have placed her in jeopardy. How could she, a member of Herod's court, so publicly associate with the cousin of John the Baptist, whom Herod had beheaded?

Joanna may have spoken to Herod and Herodias about how Jesus had transformed her life, and she may have had to leave the court to follow Jesus as his disciple. The Bible doesn't say. It must have taken enormous courage for her to follow Jesus, seeking first his kingdom rather than her own safety and comfort. But that's what love propelled her to do.

- Joanna's discipleship seems to have begun when Jesus healed her. What does her example say about the dynamics of discipleship? How are those dynamics expressed in your own life?

- What social, political, or personal risks may God be asking you to take as you seek to follow Jesus?

Father, I'm both inspired and convicted by Joanna's dedication. Show me how I can live my life fully devoted to you and your Son. Then give me courage to follow the path you've revealed.

WEEK 44

THE SYROPHOENICIAN WOMAN

Her Story

Because she displayed great faith, Jesus healed her daughter.

Jesus said to her, "Woman, you have great faith! Your request is granted." MATTHEW 15:28

READ

Matthew 15:21–28; Mark 7:24–30

Who WAS SHE?

A Canaanite mother knelt in distress before Jesus. She showed her deeper understanding of who he was by calling him "Son of David" (Matthew 15:22). Strangely, Jesus ignored her. When his disciples grew aggravated with her cries for her daughter's healing, they urged Jesus to send her away. She pleaded with Jesus for a mere "crumb" of compassion (verse 27). Recognizing her deep faith, Jesus turned to her in sympathy and healed her daughter.

A *Closer Look* AT THE SYROPHOENICIAN WOMAN'S STORY

HER STORY TOOK PLACE AROUND AD 29–30.

Soon after the death of his cousin John, Jesus miraculously fed five thousand people with five loaves of bread and two fish (Matthew 14:13-21). He then proceeded to walk on water (Matthew 14:22-33) and then sparred with a group of Pharisees about what makes someone clean or unclean (Matthew 15:1-20). Next, Jesus traveled in secret to the region of Tyre, a pagan area on the eastern coast of the Mediterranean, perhaps hoping for a time of much needed rest. But even there his fame as a healer preceded him.

When the Syrophoenician woman discovered Jesus was nearby, she hailed him, saying, "Lord, Son of David, have mercy on me!" (Matthew 15:22). Amazing that she, an "unclean" Gentile and a woman, had the temerity to speak to him, calling him "Lord" and then using a title with clear Messianic overtones. Jewish rabbis wouldn't even talk to their wives in public, let alone foreign women. Yet she addressed Jesus freely, pouring out her anguish because her daughter was possessed by a demon and suffering terribly.

Jesus responded with complete silence, which seemed to embolden his disciples, who urged him to send her away. Instead of dismissing her, he stated that he was sent only to the lost sheep of Israel. Refusing to give up, she threw herself at him, kneeling at his feet and imploring his help. But instead of being moved to pity, Jesus responded by comparing her to a dog, a derogatory term used by Jews for Gentiles.

At that point, any self-respecting Gentile would have turned on her heel and stalked out, but this woman was desperate, humble, and full of faith. Determined to help her daughter, she persisted, leveraging the insult by arguing that even dogs eat the crumbs that fall from their master's table. And it was only crumbs she was asking.

"The language Jesus uses is very strong," Kenneth Bailey explains. "Dogs in Middle Eastern traditional culture, Jewish and non-Jewish, are almost as despised as pigs. Pigs are worse, but only slightly. . . . Neglecting a beggar is one thing. But to insult her with such language is something else."[16] So why did Jesus speak so harshly?

16 Bailey, *Jesus Through Middle Eastern Eyes*, 224.

Bailey's answer is that Jesus was testing the woman and instructing his disciples at the same time. Displaying humility, faith, boldness, and persistence, she passed the test with flying colors. "Woman, you have great faith!" Jesus lauded her, granting her request (Matthew 15:28). The same was not true of the disciples. Jesus' interactions with her were like a mirror reflecting their prejudices against Gentiles and against women, upending their ideas of who was clean and who was unclean.

As Ben Witherington III points out, "Her great faith contrasts with the disciples' great annoyance at her persistent pleading. How surprised Matthew's audience must have been to hear this Gentile woman's faith called great, when a characteristic description of Jesus' own disciples in that Gospel is that they have little faith."[17]

17 Witherington III, *Women and the Genesis of Christianity* 76.

THE SYROPHOENICIAN WOMAN'S *Legacy* IN SCRIPTURE

READ

Matthew 15:21-28

- What made this woman so tenacious in her interaction with Jesus?
- What purpose might Jesus have had when he initially ignored her?
- What do you think of the disciples' reaction to her insistence?

- Jesus seemed to be testing her faith when he called her a "dog" (verse 26). Why did she react as she did, and why were crumbs enough for her?

- Where do you need persistence in your faith today? How might this woman's persistence encourage you?

OUR *Connection* TO THE SYROPHOENICIAN WOMAN

In the cultural context of the day, it would have been more common for a child's father rather than mother to seek help from someone outside the family. That was the case when the synagogue leader Jairus pleaded for Jesus to heal his daughter (Mark 5:21-43). That the Syrophoenician woman went by herself to Jesus may mean she was a widow or an unwed mother. Perhaps her daughter was all she had in the world. Her story is one of unforgettable love and more than enough faith to move mountains.

- Sometimes we don't know what is in our hearts until they've been tested. In what ways has your heart been tested, and what did you discover from this testing?

- Hebrews 11:6 says that "without faith it is impossible to please God." Explore the connection between faith and our ability to please God. Describe a time when your level of faith was high. What happened?

Lord Jesus, increase my faith in you. Give me determination like this woman's when I come to you with desperate pleas. Crumbs are enough for me, for I know that even these can make me whole.

WEEK 45

MARTHA

HER NAME IS GREEK. DERIVED FROM THE FEMININE FORM OF THE ARAMAIC WORD FOR "LORD," IT MEANS "LADY"—ESSENTIALLY, THE ONE WHO IS IN CHARGE.

Her Story

A close friend of Jesus and a hospitable woman, she grew frustrated and impatient when her sister chose to sit with the men rather than help her prepare food.

But Martha was distracted by all the preparations that had to be made. LUKE 10:40

READ

Luke 10:38-42; John 11:1-12:11

Who WAS SHE?

Criticizing her sister, Martha urged Jesus to tell Mary to help her. When he and his companions had descended on their home, an enormous job had descended on Martha. She—perhaps frantically—started all the preparations involved in feeding such a group of men, no small task. But rather than working with an eye toward serving Jesus, she grew frustrated, not with the work but with her sister. When she brought her frustration to Jesus, he gently taught her a lesson in prioritizing the one important thing.

A Closer Look AT MARTHA'S STORY

HER STORY TOOK PLACE AROUND AD 27–30.

John 11:5 says that Jesus loved Martha, Mary, and their brother, Lazarus. This is the context in which to unpack the story for which Martha has become famous.

While Martha was in the kitchen preparing a meal for Jesus and his disciples, Mary was sitting with the men, listening as Jesus spoke. In a world that expected her to be in the kitchen with Martha, Mary's choice would be seen as surprising and unconventional, even offensive. Though Jewish women were expected to provide hospitality and service, they were careful about mingling with men who weren't members of their family, so much so that unless no servants were there, they wouldn't even serve meals when unrelated men were present.

Countless sermons have been preached about Martha and her complaint against her sister, Mary. Most listeners, especially women, will harbor a secret sympathy for Martha, whom Jesus gently chided for worrying about many things. But feeding and perhaps housing so many men would have meant there was an enormous amount of work to do. Food had to be procured and prepared. The house had to be cleaned and sleeping arrangements made. Why didn't Jesus simply thank Martha for all her hard work and encourage Mary to help her? Because, like many of the narratives in the gospel, the story is about more than it seems.

One key is found in how Luke's Gospel characterizes Mary, letting the reader know that she "sat at the Lord's feet" (Luke 10:39). The phrase "to sit at the feet of" was an idiom for being the disciple of a rabbi. Paul, for instance, said he was "educated at the feet of Gamaliel" (Acts 22:3 ESV). In Martha's world, it was nearly unheard of for a woman to become the formal disciple of a rabbi who was not her husband. But here was Mary, acting just like one. Jesus praised her, saying, "Mary has chosen what is better, and it will not be taken away from her" (Luke 10:42).

In addition to needing help in the kitchen, Martha might also have been scandalized by Mary's behavior. What would the neighbors think if they found out how her little sister was behaving?

She must have been startled by Jesus' response, because he said that the most important thing was not cooking the food, milking the goat, or sweeping the house. The critical thing was to follow him, to become his wholehearted disciple. He wasn't the only rabbi to emphasize the paramount importance of discipleship. But this kind of discipleship was restricted to men. In calling a woman to practice it, Jesus started a religious revolution of sorts, affirming women's equal status and calling in the new covenant.

Jesus didn't belittle Martha's hospitality but affirmed Mary's choice and then invited Martha, whom he loved, to prioritize following him above everything. Rather than denigrating her, he elevated her as someone worthy of following him with all her heart, her mind, and her soul.

MARTHA'S *Legacy* IN SCRIPTURE

READ

Luke 10:38-42

- When have you felt like Martha or acted like her? Describe the circumstances and how you dealt with them.

- When have you chosen, like Mary, to step away and listen? Often? Rarely? Explain.

- Jesus said Martha was "worried and upset about many things" (verse 41). What might Jesus have meant? What else may have been bothering Martha in addition to her sister's lack of help? What does his statement reveal about Jesus' knowledge of Martha (and of you)?

- How do you balance the pressures and requirements of your busy life with the need to pause in order to learn from and listen to Jesus?

OUR *Connection* TO MARTHA

Martha offers a dynamic portrait of discipleship. In the scene from Luke's Gospel, we meet her as an honest, capable, hospitable, and stressed-out woman. But Jesus gently shifted her energy away from anxiety and toward listening, because, as some commentators have remarked, true discipleship always begins with listening. In the Bible, a call to listen is also a call to believe and obey.

By the time we meet her again, after her brother, Lazarus, died but before he was raised (John 11:25-27), she stands taller because of her ringing declaration of faith. For that, some have called her a theologian in her own right, anticipating what Mary Magdalene would soon do at Jesus' tomb when she became the first witness to the resurrection.

- Why is listening the first step to true discipleship? To whom and to what do you listen in your quest to follow Jesus? (Be as honest as possible about what shapes you.)

- How might Martha's story serve as a model for believing in Jesus' faithfulness when resurrection hasn't yet come?

Jesus, I freely admit to being more similar to Martha than I'd like, too busy with everything to spend time at your feet. Expand my heart until my first desire isn't to get everything done but to simply be with you.

WEEK 46

MARY OF BETHANY

HER NAME MAY MEAN "BITTERNESS" OR "BELOVED."

Her Story

Mary of Bethany not only sat at Jesus' feet to listen to him but also anointed his feet to worship him.

Mary took about a pint of pure nard, an expensive perfume; she poured it on Jesus' feet and wiped his feet with her hair. JOHN 12:3

READ

Matthew 26:6-13; Mark 14:3-9; Luke 10:38-42; John 11:1-12:11

Who WAS SHE?

Mary is always paired with Martha in the Gospels. Often juxtaposed one against the other, Martha busied herself with preparations and serving (Luke 10:40; John 12:2) while Mary could be found at Jesus' feet (Luke 10:39; John 12:3). Mary's desire to listen intently to Jesus and then to worship him extravagantly reminds us of the importance of both in our Christian walk. We listen. We learn. We worship.

A *Closer Look* AT MARY OF BETHANY'S STORY

HER STORY TOOK PLACE AROUND AD 27–30.

Mary, Martha, and Lazarus lived two miles from Jerusalem in the small village of Bethany. Among Jesus' closest friends, their home was probably a frequent stop-over whenever he was in the area.

In Luke's Gospel, Mary is depicted as Jesus' disciple. In John's Gospel, the setting and the mood shift from one of warm hospitality to one of tension and grave danger. Jesus had been staying a safe distance from Jerusalem, where hostility was swirling among the religious leaders who opposed him. That's when he received a message from Mary and Martha that their brother, Lazarus, was ill. Jesus' response is surprising: "Now Jesus loved Martha and her sister and Lazarus. So when he heard that Lazarus was sick, he stayed where he was two more days" (John 11:5-6). What? How is it possible to connect love with his deliberate delay?

When Jesus finally arrived in Bethany, Lazarus had been in the tomb four days. At that time many people believed a soul hovered near the body for three days after death in hopes of reentering it. So this was well past the possibility of resuscitation.

Unlike her sister, who is portrayed in both Luke's and John's Gospels as conversing freely with Jesus, Mary says little, uttering only one sentence in the New Testament: "Lord, if you had been here, my brother would not have died" (John 11:32). Moved by her tears, Jesus began to weep.

When he ordered the stone rolled from Lazarus's tomb, Martha pointed out that the body would stink, but Jesus replied, "Did I not tell you that if you believe, you will see the glory of God?" (John 11:40). What happened next was truly glorious—a dead man walking out of his tomb! But Jesus' own death, which would happen in just a few days' time, would explode everything human beings thought they knew about how the world works—about power, love, and the path to glory. By submitting to his Father's will, Jesus would be raised from the dead and seated at the right hand of God, reigning in glory forever.

Before this happened, Jesus attended a dinner in his honor. The resurrected Lazarus reclined at a table with Jesus and the other guests. Martha was serving while Mary poured expensive nard over Jesus' feet. Worth a year's wages, the nard, which would have come from the Himalayas, may have been Mary's dowry.

It must have seemed a fitting gift for this loving, powerful man.

Of the Mary and Martha duo, Mary was the silent one. But her gesture still speaks. How true the words of Jesus, who said about her after Judas criticized her: "Why are you bothering this woman? She has done a beautiful thing to me. . . . When she poured this perfume on my body, she did it to prepare me for burial. Truly I tell you, wherever this gospel is preached throughout the world, what she has done will also be told, in memory of her" (Matthew 26:10, 12–13).

MARY OF BETHANY'S *Legacy* IN SCRIPTURE

READ

John 11:1–44

- Compare the two parts of the sentence in John 11:6. Why would Jesus wait?

- When Jesus arrived after Lazarus's death, Martha and then Mary greeted Jesus with exactly the same words. However, he had a theological discussion with Martha, but with Mary he was "deeply moved" and "troubled" (John 11:33). What do these two interactions tell you about Martha and Mary and their relationships with Jesus?

- Mary and Martha experienced "the glory of God" (John 11:40) when Lazarus walked out of his grave. What do you think that was like? How was it evidence of God's glory?

READ

John 12:1-8

- What motivation caused Mary to take her jar of expensive perfume and let it run out all over Jesus' feet? What was she doing? How much of its significance do you think she understood?

- Discuss Jesus' rebuke of Judas when Judas belittled Mary and her act. How much of Jesus' statements about his death and burial did the disciples understand?

- What sort of lavish acts of worship might you present to Jesus?

OUR *Connection* TO MARY OF BETHANY

Mary and her family may have been among Jesus' wealthy patrons. The evidence for this includes the fact that their home was capable of hosting large gatherings and that Mary possessed such expensive perfume. Unlike Jesus' other disciples, notably Peter (Matthew 16:21–23), Mary seems to have accepted the fact that the path to glory led through Jesus' crucifixion. By wiping his feet with her hair and anointing him for burial, she expressed her complete agreement with the plan of God, a plan that none of the other disciples embraced.

- How do Mary's embodied responses to Jesus contrast with Martha's verbal confession of faith? What might this imply about different ways of perceiving and responding to Jesus?

- Mary expressed her emotions honestly, and that moved Jesus to tears. How does his weeping affect your notion of who he is and how he might respond to your own raw emotions?

- How might Mary's model of discipleship shape the way you follow Jesus?

Jesus, Messiah and King, I'm in awe of Mary's extravagance, but I feel like I have so little to offer. Perhaps I simply offer what I do have, the full devotion of my heart.

WEEK 47

SALOME

MOTHER OF THE SONS OF ZEBEDEE

"PEACE"

Her Story

She grasped for positions of influence and power for her sons in the kingdom she believed Jesus was about to rule, not knowing the implications of her request.

[Salome] said, "Grant that one of these two sons of mine may sit at your right and the other at your left in your kingdom." MATTHEW 20:21

READ

Matthew 20:20-28; 27:56; Mark 15:40-41; 16:1-2

Who WAS SHE?

Today she might be called a "Tiger Mom." Salome wasn't going to stand by and let the other disciples get ahead of her two sons. She wanted only the best for them in Jesus' kingdom. Perhaps she had pushed James and John to secure a prime position. Or they may have pushed her to speak on their behalf. Jesus didn't seem surprised by her request, but his answer revealed how little she understood about the nature of Jesus' future kingdom and what her sons would face as part of it.

A *Closer Look* AT SALOME, MOTHER OF THE SONS OF ZEBEDEE'S STORY

HER STORY TOOK PLACE AROUND AD 27–30.

Early in his ministry, Jesus moved to Capernaum, a fishing village on the Sea of Galilee. There a man named Zebedee, the husband of Salome, owned a fishing business.

Though the gospel doesn't say so, Salome's role might have included mending nets; preparing food for the workers; helping to clean, salt, or dry the fish; and selling fish in the local market. Perhaps she also kept track of finances. Her labor may have reminded us of the woman depicted in Proverbs 31.

Her two sons, James and John, were in the middle of mending nets when Jesus called them to become his disciples. Even though they stood to inherit a prosperous business, they immediately dropped their nets and followed him. Eventually Salome became Jesus' disciple too.

Matthew 20:21 depicts her in Jerusalem pleading for a special favor: "Grant that one of these two sons of mine may sit at your right hand and the other at your left in your kingdom." Like everyone else, she thought Jesus was on the verge of establishing an earthly kingdom. When that day arrived, she wanted both of her sons to occupy places of honor.

Jesus soon put her to rights.

The next time we see her, she is standing at his cross and then at his empty tomb. Though all but one of Jesus' male disciples had fled (Salome's son John was the exception), she and other faithful women bravely stood vigil as Jesus died an agonizing death. But why did the men run away?

Crucifixion was a horror show—a theater for terror devised to prevent anyone from defying Roman authority. If Jesus' male disciples had stayed at the cross, they would have risked arrest and execution. Women were rarely crucified, though when Rome wanted to subdue a population, they crucified men, women, and sometimes even children. Since women weren't usually considered a political threat, it would have been less dangerous for them. They would have been seen as mourners rather than rabble-rousers. Even so, they could have been subject to harassment, beatings, arrest, and, at the least, the loss of family honor—the very thing Salome had earlier been so eager to secure.

The morning after Jesus' death, Salome, Mary Magdalene, and Mary the mother of James brought spices to anoint Jesus' body. How amazed they must have been that instead of encountering a dead Messiah, they met an angel who told them Jesus had risen!

Later, reflecting on the fact that one rebel was crucified on Jesus' right while another was crucified on his left, Salome may have recalled her own petition that Jesus would favor her sons with positions of honor. Her experience of witnessing both Jesus' death and his resurrection must have transformed her, strengthening her for the days ahead when Herod would execute her son James (Acts 12:2) and the Emperor Domitian would exile her son John to the island of Patmos (Revelation 1:9).

SALOME, MOTHER OF THE SONS OF ZEBEDEE'S *Legacy* IN SCRIPTURE

READ

Matthew 20:20-28

- What did Jesus mean when he said that Salome didn't know what she was asking?

- Define the "cup" Jesus mentioned in his response to Salome.

- What made the other disciples "indignant" (verse 24)? How did Jesus redefine leadership?

- How might Salome have had to reimagine her sons' success and perhaps even her own? How did her interpretation of success clash with what Jesus taught?

- How do Jesus' words in Matthew 20:26–27 cause you to reimagine what is important in your own life? What drives you? What is more important for you and your children than success?

OUR *Connection* TO SALOME, MOTHER OF THE SONS OF ZEBEDEE

Salome's life is a study in discipleship. She must have been amazed when her sons abandoned the family business to follow Jesus. But later she also became Jesus' follower, one of several women, including Joanna, who traveled with him and his disciples, supplying their needs from her own purse (Luke 8:3). Even so, she displayed a common misunderstanding about his kingship and the demands of discipleship. The courage she showed at the cross and the love she revealed when traveling to the tomb to anoint Jesus' mutilated body with spices showed her rapid maturation as a disciple who would let nothing stand in the way of serving him.

- Discipleship can have both short and prolonged periods of growth. Describe the emotional and spiritual changes Salome may have experienced during the week of Jesus' passion.

- What might a graph of your own spiritual growth look like? Describe a time when you remained faithful to Jesus during difficulty.

Jesus, make me more like you! My human nature drives me toward success and recognition. Help me to become a servant to those around me. May the fruit of your Spirit within me make me more and more like you.

WEEK 48

THE WIDOW WITH THE TWO COINS

Her Story

Jesus used the widow as a living illustration to warn his disciples about hypocritical and greedy religious leaders.

A poor widow came and put in two very small copper coins, worth only a few cents. MARK 12:42

READ

Mark 12:38-44; Luke 20:45-21:4

Who WAS SHE?

Unaware that Jesus was using her to teach his disciples a lesson, the widow dropped her two small coins into the temple offering box. Though her gift seemed insignificant, Jesus said it was "all she had to live on" (Mark 12:44), making it more valuable than any of the other gifts. What a sharp contrast to the religious leaders whose faith was a show! This widow gave from her heart, trusting God to take care of her. Unlike her, the religious leaders Jesus warned against were only interested in enriching themselves by exploiting the vulnerable, especially widows.

A *Closer Look* AT THE WIDOW WITH THE TWO COINS' STORY

HER STORY TOOK PLACE AROUND AD 30, PERHAPS FOUR DAYS BEFORE THE CRUCIFIXION.

In his wonderful book *Jesus Through Middle Eastern Eyes*, Kenneth Bailey points out that Jesus had female as well as male disciples and that this influenced both the content and style of his teaching.[18] Jesus taught in a way that would deeply impact his female followers, sometimes tailoring stories and examples that would especially resonate with them. Here are a few examples:

1. The parable of the woman who found the lost coin (Luke 15:8–10)
2. The parable of the ten virgins (Matthew 25:1–13)
3. The parable of the woman leavening dough to make bread (Matthew 13:33)
4. The story of the widow with the two coins (Luke 21:1–4)

In several cases, Luke's Gospel includes paired parables that appealed to both men and women, e.g., Luke 5:36–39, which is about garment patching (traditionally women's work) and winemaking (traditionally men's work). This pairing prompted one New Testament scholar to observe, "Luke expresses by this arrangement that man and woman stand together and side by side before God. They are equal in honor and grace; they are endowed with the same gifts and have the same responsibilities."[19]

Though the story of the Widow with the Two Coins has often been used by pastors to encourage generous giving, most Bible commentators believe this was not Jesus' intent. To understand why, it's important to note that in both Mark's and

18 Bailey, *Jesus Through Middle Eastern Eyes*. 194.

19 Helmut Flender, *St Luke—Theologian of Redemptive History* (London: S.P.C.K., 1967), 10, as quoted in Witherington III, *Women and the Genesis of Christianity* 201.

Luke's Gospels, her story is sandwiched between two other important scenes. In the one immediately preceding it, Jesus was teaching in the temple courts when he cautioned his listeners against the teachers of the Law who "devour widows' houses," saying that such "men will be punished most severely" (Mark 12:40).

Right after that comes the scene in which the impoverished widow puts two coins into the temple treasury—everything she had.

In the very next scene, as Jesus and his disciples were leaving the temple, he prophesied the temple's coming destruction, saying, "Not one stone here will be left on another; every one will be thrown down" (see Matthew 24:1-2).

Instead of simply extolling the widow's incredible generosity, making it an example everyone should follow, the story is a lament. The temple, which was designed as a sacred heaven and earth space where a loving God would dwell among his people, was being corrupted by unloving and unscrupulous men who cloaked their activities in religious garb. For this, Jesus foresaw judgment. Forty years later, in AD 70, the Romans burned the temple, destroying its core structures. Tragically, the Roman Colosseum was partially financed by plunder taken from the demolished Jerusalem temple.

THE WIDOW WITH THE TWO COINS' *Legacy* IN SCRIPTURE

READ

Mark 12:38-44; Luke 20:45-21:4

What did Jesus mean when he said they "devour widow's houses" (Mark 12:40)?

- Beyond the size of their gifts, what did Jesus note was different about these givers? What did he want his disciples to understand about the widow and the teachers of the law who preyed on women like her?

- The rich in this story gave without it impacting their way of life. In contrast, how would you describe the widow's gift? What might be the consequences for her?

- Does giving like this widow did—offering the last bit you have to your name—seem to you like faith or folly? Was Jesus telling his followers to give away everything they had, or was there another point he was making?

- When has your giving been truly sacrificial? Describe the circumstances. If you've never given as an act of sacrifice, try to discover why.

OUR *Connection* TO THE WIDOW WITH THE TWO COINS

A close reading of her story reveals a deeply pious woman who was being taken advantage of by the religious hypocrites of her day. She may have gone unnoticed by those around her. But Jesus saw her, instantly understanding her condition and the forces at work that made her destitute. He also noted something important—she had given a much larger gift than the wealthy who were putting far more into the temple treasury. Just as a unit of platinum is far heavier than a unit of tin, her two coins were far weightier than every other gift.

- Who do you tend to ignore? Who might the Holy Spirit invite you to begin "seeing" and helping?

- Have you noticed ways in which your faith community is neglecting or perhaps unintentionally hurting the vulnerable? How can you pray for and urge change?

- If you feel unseen by others, how might this story encourage you?

Jesus, you are the only One who sees me deeply. Please reveal my hidden motivations and my deepest needs. Shape me so that I can be the person you want me to be—not relying on pretense, greed, or falsehoods to get my way.

WEEK 49

MARY MAGDALENE

HER NAME MAY MEAN "BITTERNESS" OR "BELOVED."

Her Story

Mary Magdalene, so named because she came from the town of Magdala, is mentioned in Scripture more often than any other woman in relation to Jesus.

When Jesus rose early on the first day of the week, he appeared first to Mary Magdalene, out of whom he had driven seven demons. MARK 16:9

READ

Matthew 27:55-56, 61; 28:1; Mark 15:40, 47; 16:1-11; Luke 8:2-3; 24:10-11; John 19:25; 20:1-18

Who WAS SHE?

Mary Magdalene entered Jesus' circle of followers after he cast demons from her, perhaps manifesting as an extreme form of mental illness. From then on, throughout the biblical narrative, she stayed close to Jesus, caring for him along with several other women. She followed Jesus so attentively that she gained a place of honor as the first to whom Jesus revealed himself after his resurrection. She was a leader in the early Christian community.

A *Closer Look* AT MARY MAGDALENE'S STORY

HER STORY TOOK PLACE AROUND AD 27–30.

Mary Magdalene is one of the Bible's most remarkable and misunderstood women. Probably hailing from the town of Magdala, on the northwest shore of the Sea of Galilee, she appears in Luke's Gospel as one of several women who traveled with Jesus after he healed them of evil spirits or illnesses (Luke 8:2).

Both Luke and Mark say that Jesus cast out seven demons from Mary. But why bother numbering them? Because in the Bible, seven is a symbolic number signifying completeness. The implication is that Mary was entirely possessed by the forces of darkness, a person beyond hope. But Jesus effected a total cleansing and a complete victory.

Unfortunately, some in the church later characterized her as a former prostitute, mistaking her for the sinful woman in Luke 7:36-50. In modern times, some have preposterously cast her in the role of Jesus' romantic partner despite the fact there is zero evidence of this.

Tellingly, Mary Magdalene is the only person explicitly named in the Bible as having witnessed three critical episodes in the gospel—Jesus' death, burial, and resurrection. Because she was a female with a challenging past, she would not have been a credible witness by anyone's standards. How in keeping with the surprising nature of Jesus' kingdom that he would choose Mary to bear witness to his world-shattering victory!

John 20:1-18 is especially important in understanding Mary's story. The preceding text (John 19:41) mentions that there was a garden at the place Jesus was crucified, and in that garden there was a tomb where his dead body was laid.

It is no accident, as Tim Mackie, N. T. Wright, and others have pointed out, that Mary's encounter with the risen Jesus took place in a garden. John's narrative is shot through with creation and garden of Eden imagery. Sin and death both began and ended in a garden.

1. Just as on the *first day* God created the heavens and the earth (Genesis 1:1), Mary arrived at Jesus' empty tomb on the *first day* of the week.
2. Just as on the first day of creation God separated light from darkness (Genesis 1:3-5), Mary peered into the empty tomb "while it was still dark," right before sunrise (John 20:1).
3. Just as God placed Adam and Eve in the garden of Eden to tend it (Genesis 2:15), Mary mistook Jesus for the gardener. In fact, he is the Gardener—the second Adam cultivating the new creation.
4. Just as the first adam (the human, not yet "Adam" in a gendered sense) named the creatures (Genesis 2:19-20), Jesus called Mary by name. That is precisely the moment she recognized him.

Mary Magdalene, completely possessed by the darkness, was completely liberated by the love and power of Jesus Christ. She was the first human being to preach the good news of Jesus' resurrection and to taste the reality of the new creation into which Jesus welcomes every man and woman who puts their faith in him.

MARY MAGDALENE'S *Legacy* IN SCRIPTURE

READ

Luke 8:2-3

- What sort of illness or problems might "seven demons" produce? What sort of reaction would Mary have had at being healed by Jesus?

- Why did Mary Magdalene and these other women follow Jesus and his disciples? Give some specifics about how they might have supported them.

READ
Matthew 27:55-56

- Why did Mary Magdalene and these other women stay to watch the terrible spectacle of Jesus' crucifixion?

READ
John 20:1-16

- When Jesus called Mary Magdalene "woman" (John 20:15), she didn't recognize him. When he called her "Mary" (John 20:16), she immediately knew he was her risen Savior. Why is this so? What was the difference?

- What does Jesus' appearance to a woman first after his resurrection tell you about how he understood the place of women in his culture then and in his church today?

OUR *Connection* WITH MARY MAGDALENE

Mary Magdalene's story assures us that there is no mental or physical illness, no addiction, no terrible prognosis that Jesus cannot defeat. Opening the door even slightly to Jesus lets in the light that can overpower the darkness.

The new creation so vividly pointed to in John 20:18 means that your past does not define your future. You are not stuck, trapped, or impossibly broken. Suffering will end, and death will not win. Like Mary, you will have a future that is full of light. Because of her transformation, Mary became one of Jesus' most devoted disciples and a significant leader in the early church.

- Where do you most identify with Mary?

- Imagine you are Mary Magdalene at Jesus' garden tomb. What do you see? What do you feel? What does Jesus say to you?

- Pray for someone you know who seems beyond hope. Let the Holy Spirit guide you.

Jesus, the beauty and power of this story touches me profoundly, making me want to be a loyal and devoted disciple, like Mary Magdalene. Thank you for calling me by my name, just as you called Mary. Give me the zeal to serve you as she did.

WEEK 50

DORCAS

HER NAME IS GREEK AND MEANS "GAZELLE."
"TABITHA" IS ITS ARAMAIC EQUIVALENT.

Her Story

Well-loved by the needy women around her, Dorcas was the first and only recorded person whom the apostle Peter raised from the dead.

A disciple named Tabitha . . . was always doing good and helping the poor. ACTS 9:36

READ

Acts 9:36-43

Who WAS SHE?

Dorcas, aka Tabitha, an early disciple of Jesus and an admirable woman, served the needy around her, and her unexpected death left a great void in the community. The needy women, primarily widows, grieved her deeply, not just as someone who helped them but as someone who loved them. When Jesus' disciple Peter arrived, they gathered around to show him the clothing Dorcas had sewn for them. Peter's simple act of kneeling and praying in faith raised Dorcas back to life and brought many to faith in Jesus.

A Closer Look AT DORCAS'S STORY

HER STORY TOOK PLACE AROUND AD 35–40.

What do you get when you combine God's power over death with a life of humble service? You get a remarkable woman named Dorcas, also known as Tabitha, who is described in the book of Acts as "always doing good" (Acts 9:36). Her story would have loomed large among the widows she served and also among those who put their faith in Jesus after hearing what happened to her.

Since her name is rendered in both Greek (Dorcas) and Aramaic (Tabitha), she may have been known to both Greek- and Aramaic-speaking communities. The only woman in the New Testament explicitly identified as a "disciple" (verse 36), hers was a life of compassionate and humble service, especially aimed at widows. Since the system favored male inheritance, widows were often left destitute. While some made their living managing a dowry or an inherited estate, others worked in textiles, baking, agriculture, the domestic sphere, or crafts. The term *widow* included not only women whose husbands had died but also divorced and unmarried women. It was broadly used for women with no male provider or protector.

These were the women who crowded, weeping and wailing, into Dorcas's home in Joppa, a town on the Mediterranean coast, just thirty-eight miles northwest of Jerusalem, near modern-day Tel Aviv. Into this atmosphere, thick with both gratitude and grief, waded the apostle Peter. He had been traveling in the region and was summoned by disciples after Dorcas's death. Their urgent plea reached him not long after he healed a paralyzed man in a nearby town.

Peter cleared the room where the dead woman lay, got down on his knees, and began to pray. Then he commanded, "Tabitha, get up" (Acts 9:40). And she did! In that moment, when Dorcas came back to life, the kingdom of God became vividly present. God, it seemed, was using Dorcas's story to emphasize that this was how he wanted his people to live. Like Dorcas, everyone was to serve with humility, be knit together in community, pray without ceasing, and share with each other generously. These were the bedrock values upon which the kingdom would rise.

How must it have felt for Dorcas to return to life and then go on living day after day? To join the small community of the resurrected—the son of the widow of Zarephath (1 Kings 17:8-24), the son of the Shunammite woman (2 Kings 4:8-37), the son of the widow of Nain (Luke 7:11-17), the daughter of Jairus (Matthew 9:18-19, 23-26), Lazarus (John 11:1-44), and Eutychus (Acts 20:7-12)? Dorcas would have been a living, breathing, walking, talking manifestation of the kingdom of light breaking into the kingdom of darkness. People became Jesus followers not only because of miracles like the one Peter performed but because of people like Dorcas whose life spoke powerfully about God's love for the least and the last. No wonder the gospel spread quickly, like sparks racing through dry grass!

Dorcas's *Legacy* in Scripture

READ

Acts 9:36-43

- Imagine you are one of the women Dorcas helped. How would you describe her?

- Point out where you first see chaos and then joy in this story. Picture the two scenes.

- When she died, Dorcas's friends remembered her for her good works and for all the ways she helped them. How do you think you will be remembered when you die? How do you want to be remembered? What should you do to make that happen?

- Dorcas used one of her talents to serve others. What talent(s) do you have that could be used for others?

- Does it ever strike you as odd that God does miraculous things for some but not for others? What does that tell you about God?

- Dorcas showed Jesus to others by the kind of life she lived. How did her death and resurrection do the same?

OUR *Connection* TO DORCAS

Though Dorcas was a devoted Jesus follower, her good works didn't give her back her life. It was the will of God acting through the prayers of Peter. Like all the other resurrected people in the Bible, except for Jesus, Dorcas would have to die again. Though good works are evidence of faith, they're not bargaining chips. Fortunately, our relationship with God is never transactional. We don't give him something to get something. Because Jesus is our brother and God is our Father, we can exult with the apostle Paul, "Where, O death, is your victory? Where, O death, is your sting?" (1 Corinthians 15:55).

- How might Dorcas's story reveal what God thinks about ordinary service, often conducted in hidden and humble ways?

- Compare her story with that of the healings performed by Elijah (1 Kings 17:7–24) and Elisha (2 Kings 4:8–37). What might we learn from their commonalities?

Lord, I thank you that you included women like Dorcas in the Bible, people who show me the way to live for others. Help me to develop the fruits of the Spirit that will enable me to live my life loving and serving those around me.

WEEK 51

LYDIA

HER NAME SIGNIFIES THAT SHE WAS FROM LYDIA, A REGION IN WESTERN ASIA MINOR.

Her Story

Lydia, a Gentile, regularly prayed and worshiped God on the Sabbath with other women, outside on a riverbank.

[Lydia] was a worshiper of God. The Lord opened her heart to respond to Paul's message. ACTS 16:14

READ

Acts 16:11-40

Who WAS SHE?

A successful businesswoman in a time when men dominated commercial enterprises, Lydia dealt in purple cloth. One Sabbath, she encountered Paul talking to the women gathered by the river for prayer. The Spirit opened her heart to accept the message of Jesus, and she and her household were baptized. A prosperous woman, Lydia opened her home to Paul and became a leader in the early church.

A *Closer Look* AT LYDIA'S STORY

HER STORY TOOK PLACE AROUND AD 46–48.

Paul and his companions were traveling in Asia Minor (modern-day Turkey), where they were mysteriously prevented by the Holy Spirit from preaching the gospel (Acts 16:6-7). One night God gave Paul a vision of a Macedonian man begging him to "come over to Macedonia and help us" (Acts 16:9).

Instead of meeting a man when he arrived in the Roman colony of Philippi, Paul met a successful businesswoman named Lydia, who would become the first baptized Christian in Europe and a founder of the church in that city. Lydia was a God-fearer (a Gentile attracted to Judaism) who encountered Paul when she gathered with other women outdoors for prayer on the Sabbath. Though Paul usually began his evangelistic efforts by preaching the gospel in the synagogues where he traveled, Philippi's Jewish population may not have been large enough to support a synagogue.

As Lydia sat on the riverbank listening to Paul preach, God "opened her heart" (Acts 16:14), and she and all the members of her household were baptized. Afterward, she invited Paul and his companions to stay with her, making her home the center of the early church in Philippi.

Acts 16:14 identifies Lydia as a "dealer in purple cloth," which meant she was a wealthy woman. The dye likely used in the cloth she sold was very difficult to extract from the murex snails that produced it. To dye a single Roman toga might require tens of thousands of shells and an enormous amount of labor. Because of its scarcity, Tyrian purple became a status symbol in the Roman Empire. Over time, only emperors or high-ranking officials could legally wear the royal purple while others wore strips of purple to indicate their rank.

Because of her trade, Lydia would have been connected to the Roman elite in her area as well as to other merchants. She may have been a widow living comfortably in a large Roman-style home, which would have included reception rooms for business associates and others, work and storage areas, a courtyard, and perhaps a garden. Whatever her home was like, it became the first house church in Europe.

Ben Witherington III points out that one of the main ways the early church grew was by entire households converting to the faith, which is what happened in Lydia's story. This also happened in Philippi when Paul's jailer and his household converted after an earthquake caused prison doors to fly open but no prisoners escaped (Acts 16:16–34). This dynamic, along with the fact that Christians often met to worship in houses, reinforced the idea that Christians are brothers and sisters in the household of God.[20]

A patron and leader of the church in Philippi, Lydia was one of the early church's most influential women, used by God to plant the gospel in Europe.

---

20 Witherington III, *Women and the Genesis of Christianity*, 181.

LYDIA'S *Legacy* IN SCRIPTURE

READ

Acts 16:6-15

- How did Lydia's worship of God play into her response to Paul's message?

- What does it mean that Lydia's heart was opened? How did that affect her response to Paul's message?

- In a similar way, John Wesley said his "heart was strangely warmed" when he experienced assurance of his salvation.[21] Have you ever had a "heart" experience with Jesus? How would you describe it?

READ

Acts 16:16-40

- What does Paul's experience in Philippi tell you about the city where Lydia lived and established a house church?

- Why do you think Lydia and the others needed encouragement from Paul (Acts 16:40)?

OUR *Connection* TO LYDIA

Paul's strategy was to go wherever the Spirit led, no matter how unlikely that place seemed. In this case, it was to a Gentile woman on the continent of Europe. In Macedonia, Lydia would have had more freedom than most other women in the empire. She could act publicly and own property. She could behave decisively and generously. She influenced her entire household, including any slaves, freed persons, apprentices, or relatives, to be baptized along with her.

---

21 John Wesley, *The Journal of John Wesley*, vol. 6, chap. 2, sec. 16, Christian Classics Ethereal Library (accessed April 21, 2026).

Like many influential women in the early church, she used her wealth and social connections to provide a basis for the church to spread and flourish. Hospitable and generous, Lydia didn't flinch from hosting the church in her home even when Paul and his companion Silas were thrown into prison.

- Lydia was praying when the gospel reached her, and God "opened her heart" (Acts 16:14). How might God want to deepen your openness to every dimension of the gospel?

- How might the Spirit be inviting you to share your gifts and resources, through hospitality and other means, to strengthen the church?

Jesus, open my heart like Lydia's to more—more of you, more of serving others with whatever you've given me. More. Always more.

WEEK 52

PRISCILLA

THE DIMINUTIVE OF "PRISCA," MEANS "WORTHY" OR "VENERABLE"

Her Story

Priscilla worked alongside her husband, Aquila, in the business of tent-making. Refugees from Rome, they had settled in Corinth, where Paul encountered them.

Priscilla and Aquila, my co-workers in Christ Jesus . . . . risked their lives for me. ROMANS 16:3–4

READ

Acts 18-19; Romans 16:3-5; 1 Corinthians 16:19; 2 Timothy 4:19

Who WAS SHE?

Distinguished for her business acumen, Priscilla provided leadership and guidance to several churches in the Roman Empire. Her encounter with the gifted teacher Apollos, and the way in which she helped him deepen his understanding of the gospel, shows her keen intellect, leadership skills, tact, and knowledge of the way of Jesus. Paul depended on Priscilla to help spread the gospel in the Roman Empire.

A *Closer Look* AT PRISCILLA'S STORY

HER STORY TOOK PLACE AROUND AD 49–67.

Priscilla and Aquila were Jewish believers expelled from Rome by the Emperor Claudius about AD 49. Like most Roman rulers, Claudius was allergic to disorder. His decree was meant to squelch arguments among Jews about the significance of Jesus. But no decree, even from the most powerful emperor on earth, could stop the lightning-fast spread of the gospel.

In Priscilla's case, the emperor's decree allowed the Holy Spirit to reposition her and her husband so that they could plant and lead churches across the empire. Leaving Rome, they moved to Corinth, where they eventually met the apostle Paul. As fellow tentmakers, they invited Paul to stay with them. Together, they would have worked with a wide variety of customers—shepherds, farmers, merchants, soldiers, and travelers—looking to purchase or repair a tent, a sail, or an awning.

Filled with bolts of wool, linen, and goat hair, the couple's workshop likely opened onto the street, allowing people to enter and conduct business. Their work was repetitive, which made conversation of all kinds possible. In many ways it was an ideal space for them and for Paul to conduct ministry. A back room or loft could have been used for living space or storage, and there may also have been an apartment above the workshop that provided additional rooms. Their home probably connected to a courtyard where tent panels could be spread out. It would have been well-suited for a house church, offering both privacy and public access. As respected artisans, Priscilla and her husband were in touch with local Jews and Gentiles as well as with travelers crisscrossing the empire.

Paul referred to both Priscilla and her husband, Aquila, as his "co-workers" (Romans 16:3). Along with him, they planted the gospel, taught, and led churches in Corinth, Ephesus, and Rome. In a culture in which name order was never random, Priscilla's name appeared before Aquila's, not once, but three times in the New Testament (Acts 18:18; Acts 18:26; Romans 16:3). It may have been a way of signaling that she was the more dynamic leader and teacher of the two.

After leaving Corinth with Paul to plant a church in Ephesus, she and Aquila remained there when Paul went to Jerusalem. In Paul's absence, a brilliant Jewish believer from Alexandria arrived in Ephesus and began to preach. His name was Apollos. Well-educated and knowledgeable in the Jewish Scriptures, he had only a partial understanding of Jesus. So, Priscilla and Aquila took him aside and taught him, enabling him to minister more effectively.

Again, Priscilla's name came first. In both Greco-Roman and Jewish culture, women would not normally be allowed to teach religious or philosophical matters to an adult male. But Acts 18:24-26 clearly states not only that Priscilla taught an adult male but also that her pupil was a distinguished leader. Like Deborah and the prophet Huldah, Priscilla upset the applecart when it came to social expectations and spiritual authority. She exercised substantial leadership in the early church.

PRISCILLA'S *Legacy* IN SCRIPTURE

READ
Acts 18:1-16

- What significance is there in the fact that Priscilla's name is often mentioned first?

- How did she and her husband, Aquila, use their home not only as a workplace but also as a place of hospitality? How might this have helped in the spread of the gospel even beyond Corinth?

READ
Acts 18:24-28

- What do you know about Alexandria? Where was it? Why was it included in the description of Apollos along with the fact that he was "a learned man" (verse 24)?

- Why do you think Priscilla and Aquila invited Apollos into their home to instruct him?

- How important do you think it is to understand the Bible? How can you continually deepen your understanding of God's Word?

READ

1 Corinthians 16:19

- What does this verse tell you about how Aquila and Priscilla worked together as husband and wife? What might that sort of cooperation look like for some husbands and wives today?

OUR *Connection* TO PRISCILLA

The gospel created many new possibilities for women, often lifting them into visible ministry roles. This was true not only of Priscilla but of Phoebe (Romans 16:1-2), Junia (Romans 16:7), Lydia (Acts 16), and Euodia and Syntyche (Philippians 4:2-3), and to many other women whose names we do not know. Beyond being a gifted leader, Priscilla must also have been a courageous woman, for Paul extols both her and Aquila for risking their lives to save him (Romans 16:3-4). Tragically, they could not rescue him when he was later martyred in Rome during Nero's persecution of Christians.

- How are Christians today being called to take risks for the sake of others? How can we discern when and how to act?

- Priscilla and Aquila worked together in both their profession and their ministry. How can their example help men and women today to collaborate in ministry?

- What about Priscilla's life inspires you the most and why?

Father, the courage of these early believers in the face of persecution and death astounds me. Give me courage to boldly tell others about you and your saving grace, no matter the consequences.

ABOUT THE AUTHORS

Ann Spangler is an award-winning author, whose books have helped millions to deepen their love and understanding of the Bible. Best-known for works such as *Praying the Names of God for 52 Weeks*, *Women of the Bible* (co-authored with Jean Syswerda), and *Sitting at the Feet of Rabbi Jesus* (co-authored with Lois Tverberg), she helps men and women find fresh approaches to reading Scripture. With a mix of careful research and engaging writing, she brings the ancient world of the Bible to life in ways that are spiritually rich, practical, and deeply personal.

Jean E. Syswerda is a former editor and associate publisher for Zondervan Bibles. During her years there, she helped produce the first editions of beloved and bestselling Bibles including the *NIV Adventure Bible* (1989) and the *NIV Teen Study Bible* (1993). She is also the author of the recently released *NIV Kingdom Girls Bible*. Jean was married to the love of her life for nearly fifty-two marvelous years before he went home to heaven. She delights in her family and often proudly shares about her three children and their spouses, nine grandchildren, and two great-granddaughters. Jean spends her summers in rural Michigan and her winters enjoying the Florida sunshine.